MOROCCO

COURTYARDS AND GARDENS

MOROCCO
COURTYARDS AND GARDENS

ACHVA BENZINBERG STEIN

THE MONACELLI PRESS

First published in the United States of America in 2007 by
The Monacelli Press, Inc.
611 Broadway, New York, New York 10012

Copyright © 2007 by The Monacelli Press, Inc.

Library of Congress Cataloging-in-Publication Data

Stein, Achva Benzinberg.
  Morocco : courtyards and gardens / Achva Benzinberg Stein.
    p. cm.
  Includes index.
  ISBN 978-1-58093-194-6 (hardcover)
  1. Courtyard gardens--Morocco. 2. Courtyards--Morocco. I. Title.
  SB473.2.S74 2007
  712.0964--dc22
                        2007028728

Printed and bound in Italy

Designed by Abigail Sturges

CONTENTS

PREFACE

The garden is the perfect human habitat. So far as there is one paradise for all men, all gardens in all times and places are alike; their peculiarities measure the unique experience of each society as it confronted nature . . . Allowed to go wild, [the garden] becomes a natural landscape. Tightly organized in a formal abstraction it reveals less of nature and more of the mental representation of spatial relationships and sculptural abstraction. —PAUL SHEPARD

Human beings affirm their existential position in the world in three ways: through their relation to themselves, through their relation to one another, and through their relation to place. Gardens are existential footholds in the physical environment, the formal expression of the considerations given to the consumption of natural resources and the manifestation of a society's particular myth regarding man's control over nature.

The physical realities of Morocco have produced specific agricultural and animal husbandry practices, as well as inventive technologies for harvesting and controlling water. These methods, in the context of limited resources and fervent religious beliefs, determine the form and content of Moroccan landscapes and gardens. Two types of "gardens" are found in Morocco: the natural and the constructed. The natural garden comes in many forms, from small to large, from forest to sand dune, from groves on fertile land to sedums clinging to bare rock. Water, the basis of all life, is central to the places where plants and animals take hold. Plants cluster in the depressions around water sources where hills and rocks can protect them from the excessive heat and drying winds. From mountains to deserts, the native flora and fauna communities are sparse and tightly organized. Since thickets are rare, most plants become objects by themselves, each individual specimen wresting enough space from others to provide for itself in its struggle for resources.

Humans borrowed the essence of the Moroccan plant communities and the way they inhabit the land and combined them with traditional agricultural practices to create the constructed gardens of Morocco. These fall into three basic types: the simple courtyard, an open area within a building that is either paved (*ouest ed-dar*) or planted (*riyad*); the extensive planted garden of the rulers and the wealthy citizens, enclosed within the dwelling but occasionally open for use by the public (grand *riyad*); and the plantation (*agdal* or *arsat*), which usually includes both groves of fruit trees and ornamental plantings. The scale and the articulation of these basic garden types depend on the status and resources of the owner. Although different in size and function, these spaces share certain features. The plants are spaced judiciously to achieve a sense of refuge while maintaining openness. Walls protect people and plants from the strong sun, the drying winds, and the eyes of the public. The organization of the space depends ultimately on the availability of water and its source, whether an opulent reservoir, a network of irrigation channels, or a simple basin for religious ablutions. The water features are further articulated by the texture, color, and the use of specific materials to create an ambience of tranquility, abundance, and seclusion.

All gardens, especially in arid and semiarid zones of the world, offer refuge from the harsh realities of daily life, a place for people to restore themselves and to contemplate the vision of paradise on earth. It is important that this vision of paradise not be restricted to places humans make for themselves, but that it be recognized and protected in the wild and cultivated land around us. Natural resources and fertile land have always been precious in Morocco, and they become scarcer every year. Open space is in demand by the ever-increasing population, putting pressure on the native plant and animal life, which now must struggle for habitat and sustenance. This pressure on the land makes it imperative that we work to maintain our natural gardens, not just create constructed ones, and that we address our need to change the natural world around us to fit transitory images of what constitutes a suitable contemporary landscape.

THE NATURAL CONTEXT

THE LAND

Oceans once engulfed the area now known as Morocco. The collision of the African, European, and American tectonic plates lifted the land and drained the ocean, creating an area now divided by great mountain ranges into five distinct regions, each differing considerably in climate and terrain. The region known as eastern Morocco encompasses the upper Moulouya River basin, the high eastern plateaus, and the Taza Pass. This pass, situated two thousand feet above sea level, separates the Rif Massif from the Middle Atlas mountain range. Throughout history, the pass has served as the principal east-west land connection from the Atlantic coastal plain to eastern Morocco and Algeria. The crest of these ranges lies close to the Mediterranean, causing the area's rivers to flow abruptly into a rocky, harborless coast.

The Rif Massif is an extension of the European Alps and the lowest and most northerly of the four great Moroccan mountain ranges. The Rif forms a rugged and impenetrable fortress like barrier from the Straits of Gibraltar to Al Hoceima. Its craggy Mediterranean side is eroded, carved by steep ravines, and sparsely covered with juniper and thuya. The southern side receives far more moisture, which encourages the plant growth that supports diverse wildlife.

The High and Middle Atlas mountains divide central Morocco in a great diagonal swath, creating a barrier between the rainy Atlantic coast and the arid Sahara Desert. These great mountain ranges form two climatic zones on either side, each dramatically different from the other. The mountains also create two separate and totally distinct geographical zones containing sheer granite cliffs, forests, volcanic plateaus, and steppe. The Middle Atlas is

the older range, comprising the central plateaus of the country south of the Rif and the Sebou River basin. This range is a combination of chalky limestone tablelands, partially covered with volcanic lava flows, craggy "folded" ravines, mountain peaks such as Bou Nasser and Bou Iblane, and collapsed stretches of land, which reveal underlying rocks and boulders.

The High Atlas, the highest mountain range in North Africa, runs to the south of the Middle Atlas, separating the paleoarctic from the subtropical regions of Morocco. The range begins as cliffs on the Atlantic coast between Essaouira and Agadir and continues northeast to the high plateau west of Bouarfa, near the eastern border with Algeria. The crest of the range lies at 13,665 feet at the peak of Mount Toubkal, the highest peak in North Africa. The landscape of the High Atlas is one of dramatic contrasts, with high snow-covered peaks; steep, narrow ravines and canyons; and broad valleys and plains.

The pre-Sahara region includes the Anti-Atlas range to the south and the stark, rocky, arid plateaus to the southeast. The Anti-Atlas Mountains parallel the High Atlas and are the most southerly of the Moroccan mountain ranges. Gentler than the other ranges, its highest point lies at Sarhro Mountain (over 8,000 feet). The Anti-Atlas range is connected to the High Atlas by the volcanic Siroua massif. At this junction, the High Atlas and the Anti-Atlas are separated by the alluvial river valley of the Oued Sous. South of the river the land is desert, with an annual rainfall of less than four inches. The land slopes gradually away to the east and south of the Anti-Atlas to the pre-Saharan desert, forming a rocky paved terrain called *hamada*. Deep ravines have

TANGIER •

• TETOUAN

• CHEFCHAOUEN

KENITRA •   SEBOU RIVER

• **RABAT**   • **FEZ**
                              • **MEKNES**
CASABLANCA •

• SAFI

• ESSAOUIRA   • **MARRAKECH**

TIZI–N–TICHKA •   • ERFOUD
          • TELOUÉT   • TAFILALT
AIT–BENHADDOU •
                    DADES VALLEY
                         • OUARZAZATE
• AGADIR

                    DRAA VALLEY

OUED DRAA

OUED MOULOUYA

Todra Gorge, near Tinerhir.

Mountain peak in the limestone plateau of the Middle Atlas.

been cut into the landscape by intermittent streams and rivers (*wadis*) flowing down from the plateau and the mountains. Saharan winds sweep through, shaping the stony desert and the rocky plateau that rises above the *hamada*. In the ravines are narrow alluvial valleys in which oases may be found. Vast sand seas (*ergs*) cover a few limited areas in the east, on the border between Morocco and Algeria.

The Atlantic coastal plain extends uninterrupted from Tangier southward along the entire length of the Atlantic coast, where most of the major cities and industry, the majority of the population, and the bulk of cultivated land are located. The Rharb Plain at the mouth of the Sebou is the most fertile agricultural region in Morocco. Beaches along the coast are flat, with abundant tidal pools rich in seaweed and marine life that attract large populations of sea birds. Even though there are no natural harbors on

Large trees on the road from Fez to Rabat are supported by a hollow where water collects.

the Atlantic coastline, the relative accessibility and the richness of the agricultural land have given it geopolitical importance, making it the target of repeated invasions. With colonization, man-made harbors were constructed along the coast, becoming the power base for Morocco's rulers. Casablanca was developed as a major port, while smaller harbors were built at Agadir, Essaouira, El Jadida, and Rabat.

Morocco is richly endowed with rivers, which are of great importance to this primarily agricultural nation, where precipitation is unreliable and droughts are frequent. The most important are the Sebou River and its tributaries, originating in the Rif Mountains, supplying about half of the country's water resources. The lower Sebou flows through the Taza Pass into a large marshy area northeast of Kenitra and southward into the richest stretches of coastal plain, supplying irrigation and hydroelectric power to the most populated and densely cultivated region of the country. Two notable rivers, the Moulouya and the Nakhla, empty into the Mediterranean. The Moulouya, through its many dams, supplies water for irrigation to the agricultural land in the eastern part of the country. A dam on the Nakhla draws water from the river to supply the town of Tetouan. Other important rivers are the Oum al Rbia, the Oued Bou Regreg, and the Tensift, all of which flow into the Atlantic. The Oum al Rbia supplies water to Casablanca, the Oued Bou Regreg serves Rabat and Salé, and the tributaries of the Tensift bring water to Marrakech. The Drâa and the Dadès are the main water sources for the pre-Saharan region around Ouarzazate, while the Ziz and the Rheris provide water in the Tafilalt region. The Saharan *wadis* originating in the Atlas Mountains flow intermittently, and even in the rainy season their waters thin out and evaporate before reaching the *hamada*.

ABOVE
*A narrow alluvial valley created by
runoff from the Anti-Atlas Mountains.*

RIGHT
River in the valley of Qued Nfiss.

FOLLOWING PAGES
*This small village maintains a precarious
existence on a volcanic plateau in the
High Atlas.*

FLORA AND FAUNA

Moroccan scenery can be described as a series of concentric circles, each radiating from a center of human settlement. This division is, of course, theoretical, and there are no lines of demarcation between the zones, but the changes from one to another are readily perceptible. From the outer circle composed of native flora to the inner circle with its imported or exotic species, the landscape is composed as a series of designed and planted gardens. Sparsely populated by vegetation in seemingly ordered fashion and in a human scale, the landscape is composed of small micro-ecological patches shaped by natural forces such as climate, the availability of water, the terrain, the composition of the soil and its parent material, and by human understanding of these constraints.

In order to sustain human habitation and at the same time let the other living things have room and provisions for survival, a delicate balance in the quest for resources needs to be maintained. This struggle is readily apparent to visitors. The panorama of human settlements, sand dunes, flat *hamada*, narrow rivers, alpine forests, enclosed valleys, and undulating fertile fields lead one to comprehend the Moroccan landscape as a tapestry, a patchwork quilt of garden plots, both natural and man-made.

Present-day Morocco contains eight major distinct vegetation types. The sparse and scrubby argan forests of the foothills of the High and Anti-Atlas mountains present quite a different picture from the towering green cedar forests of the Rif and the High and Middle Atlas mountains, which are different again from the barren moonscape of the arid *hamada* to the south.

In the northeastern and central part of the country, from the coastal plain into the mountainous areas of the High Atlas, Mediterranean forest predominates. There are three different Mediterranean forest subtypes—broad-leaved sclerophyllous ("hard-leaved") forest, coniferous forest, and deciduous forest. Three oak species—holm oak, cork oak, and Kermes oak—dominate the broad-leaved sclerophyllous forests. Holm oak (*Quercus ilex*) is the most abundant tree species in the Mediterranean region, being very tolerant of different soils and of variations in temperature and rainfall. Cork oak (*Quercus suber*) forests are common in the western Mediterranean region. In Morocco, they are found mostly around the northern coastal plains and in some areas of the interior Rif and Middle Atlas. The cork oak forests play an important part in the nation's economy. Every nine years, the outer bark of mature trees is stripped to harvest the natural cork for sale. Kermes oak (*Quercus coccifera*) forests are found in Morocco almost exclusively in the Rif, on a wide range of soil types and rainfall zones.

Coniferous forests constitute nearly half of the Mediterranean forest in North Africa, usually in the medium and higher elevations of mountainous regions. In Morocco, eight different major variations of this forest type are present, each defined by a dominant conifer: Phoenician juniper (*Juniperus phoenicea*); Atlas cypress (*Cupressus atlantica*); Berber thuya (*Tetraclinis articulata*); Aleppo pine (*Pinus halepensis*); Atlas cedar (*Cedrus atlantica*); Moroccan fir (*Abies pinsapo marocana*); Incense juniper (*Juniperus thurifera*); and Cluster pine (*Pinus pinaster*).

The third subtype, the Mediterranean deciduous forest, forms small stands throughout northern Africa in the more humid areas. Portuguese oak (*Quercus faginea*) and Pyrenean oak (*Quercus pyrenaica*) predominate.

RIGHT
Hillsides in the Rharb region are dotted with olive trees, and bottomlands are planted with grain.

BELOW
Cork oak (Quercus suber) *in the Mamora Forest.*

The low shrubby growth of Mediterranean bushland and shrubland covers large parts of the country. Bushland, open stands of shrubs between three and seven meters tall, is found in areas that have been intensively cultivated for many hundreds of years. As a result, there is no clear consensus on what the "natural" climax state of the vegetation would be. Some scientists speculate that left undisturbed, these areas would be bushland or scrub forest dominated by olive (*Olea europaea*) and mastic tree (*Pistacia lentiscus*). Today, these semi-arid landscapes are cov-

ered by thickets of large shrubs and small trees, with a rich herb layer blanketing the understory. Where the land has been disturbed or where fields lie fallow, flowering poppies and other annuals cover the fields in spring, creating a canvas bright with contrasting reds, blues, greens, and yellows. Shrubland is similar to bushland, except the vegetation stands less than two meters tall. This cover occurs naturally in the harsh climate and thin soils of the upper reaches of the High and Middle Atlas, giving rise to a landscape of low, round, often spiny dwarf shrubs. Like bush-

land, it also occurs as secondary growth in areas whose normal vegetation has been lost to deforestation, overuse, or other environmental degradation.

Argan scrub forest and bushland, a dominant vegetation type of southwest Morocco, is found at the lower elevations of the foothills of the High Atlas and Anti Atlas mountains between Agadir, Essaouira, and Ouarzazate. The argan (*Argania spinosa*) is a multi-stemmed tree and a valuable resource in the harsh climate. The nuts are harvested for their oil, while goats browse upon the leaves, sometimes climbing into the canopy for a meal. Most argan forests today have been overtaken by agriculture and are now effectively open orchards, with crops planted between trees, or treed pastures where goats are set out to browse. In wetter areas, the trees can produce a forest canopy up to ten meters tall; in arid regions, the argan becomes stunted and creates a scrubby bushland.

Morocco gum/lotus jujube bushland was once common on the dry plains of the Haouz-Tadla around Marrakech. The orig-

Argan tree.

*Field of wild poppies on the road
between Rabat and Casablanca.*

inal plant community, comprised primarily of Morocco gum (*Acacia gummifera*) and lotus jujube (*Ziziphus lotus*), although degraded, can still be found in a few isolated pockets, but most of its range has been taken over by extensive agricultural development of the land.

Water-conserving succulent plants dominate the dry and low-lying semi-arid parts of southwestern Morocco, thriving especially in windy places near the ocean that receive occasional moisture from sea mists. Depending on specific microclimates, different kinds of euphorbia will dominate particular locations. Groves of officinal spurge (*Euphorbia resinifera*) can be found on shallow soils in the foothills of the Atlas Mountains near Beni Mellal. At first the land appears to be half euphorbia and half bare rock, with a few trees dotted sparsely around the landscape. Closer inspection reveals small herbaceous plants tucked among the euphorbia. Two other euphorbias, King Juba's euphorbia (*Euphorbia res-jubae*) and Beaumier's euphorbia (*Euphorbia beaumierana*) often occur together as sparse cover on rocky slopes and cliff tops in coastal areas between Agadir and Safi, but one or the other may dominate in particular locations. South of Agadir, Euphorbia echinus communities colonize the region's arid, rocky hillsides and stony foothills.

In the transitional zones between the Mediterranean climate and the Sahara desert, great stretches of grassy vegetation dominate the landscape. Large reeds surround the mouths of rivers, sheltering migratory birds. *Stipa tenacissima*, known as alfa or es-

Sagebrush, alpha grass, and euphorbia tuffets.

parto grass, is an important resource for the residents of the area. Scientists are still debating whether these grasslands represent the climax communities of the region or whether they are secondary to the destruction of the native forest communities. The dry, high plateaus of southern Morocco contain vast stretches of Esparto grass and sparte (*Lygeum spartum*), with occasional patches of low-growing artemisia shrubland. These grasslands provide important grazing for sheep and goats during the rainy season. Although there are some small plants found in the herb layer on the treeless high plateau, in many degraded places esparto grass will be the only species present.

In the Moroccan desert and across the dunes, strong westerly winds sculpt the land and plants to create a series of minimalist gardens. Here the struggle for life and sustenance is manifested in the size, shape, form, and texture of the elements that compose the spaces. The Moroccan desert is not a monolithic landscape. *Hamada* desert is flat, wind-swept, and rocky. Although these desert plateaus are mostly devoid of vegetation, some plants are able to grow in the low hollows and crevices of the stony pavement where water collects. Hardy species of *Fredolia*, *Limoniastrum*, and *Reseda* are capable of surviving in these marginal environments. *Ergs* are large sandy desert areas, often with great dunes created by the wind and moving sands. While shifting dunes are sterile, more stable dunes can support particularly tenacious vegetation, such as the grass *Stipagrostis pungens* and the shrub *Cornulaca monacantha*. *Regs* are stony deserts, strewn with gravel and broken rock. The surface gravel can be so dense that roots cannot penetrate, and such desert will be devoid of vegetation. In places with some sandy cover, such as drainage channels, varieties of *Stipagrostis*, *Fredolia*, and *Haloxylon* may dot the ground.

Desert areas have intermittent streams, or *wadis*, that are the result of thunderstorms in distant headwater regions. These ephemeral streams are generally loaded with silt and sand, although a few streams cut into impervious rock run throughout the year. *Wadis* have potential for torrential flash flooding and range in size from small gullies to large, broad valleys and deep canyons. *Wadis* are the only desert landscapes (except for oases) that have sufficient water to support trees and large shrubs. In

sandy *wadis* near the southern mountain massifs, where the water table is within seven or eight meters of the surface, thickets of *Tamarix gallica* can be found. Because the water drains into the desert from the Atlas Mountains, it often brings seeds of northern species with it, such as *Nerium oleander*, *Populus euphratica*, and *Vitex agnus-castus*, which then colonize the edges of the *wadis*. Thorny acacia trees, such as *Acacia tortilis*, can also be found along these ephemeral watercourses.

Oases occur in the open desert or at the foot of the mountains above naturally occurring underground watercourses. The water— whether abundant or only a seasonal trickle—creates a garden within the dry expanse of the desert. These garden spots are now cultivated with crops of cereals, vegetables, and fruits that sustain villages. Between the reeds and sandbanks along the fertile strip of the Sous Messa, there are many such cultivated gardens.

In the arid interior of the Western Sahara and to the south of the High Atlas Mountains, oasis subsistence agriculture has supported the population for many centuries. Along the bank of the Ziz River, ribbons of garden plots composed of olive trees, date palms, cereals, and alfalfa run for miles, extending from the southern slopes of Jebel Ayash to the Tafilalt alluvial plain. These plains are home to the most important palm groves in Morocco, known as palmeries, the descendants of a very ancient agricultural tradition of tiered planting that originated in Egypt four thousand years ago. Under this system, plants of different heights are grown together in the same plot. The palm trees provide shade for more delicate fruit trees, while vegetables and field crops grow on the ground beneath. In these productive gardens, almonds, figs, apricots, pomegranates, and grapevines are cultivated for both personal use and for the market. Alfalfa, barley, wheat, and vegetables such as tomatoes, cabbage, and onions are also cultivated for domestic consumption, while roses are grown for their oil and perfume.

The date palm (*Phoenix dactylifera*) originated in the Indus Valley and was subsequently brought to Mesopotamia, Iran, the Nile Valley, the arid areas of the Mediterranean, and North Africa. Arab tradition refers to the date as the tree of life in the Garden of Eden, and the trees are mentioned many times in the Koran and the Old Testament. The generic name of the plant may have been de-

Desert oasis with date palms and field crops in Ouarzazate.

rived from the phoenix, the fiery bird of Greek mythology. Other researchers say that the name of the palm came from "Phoenician"—the people who spread the tree around the Arab world, with the bird receiving its name from the tree.

The plant is dioecious, having separate male and female trees. While the tree can grow in the heat of the desert, it requires irrigation; it will tolerate water with a very high salt content. Mature palms need about seventy liters of water every ten days in the winter and seventy liters every two days in the summer. A common expression has it that "a palm has to have its feet in the water and its head in fire."

Date palms can reach a height of twelve meters or more and mature between thirty and eighty years of age. The tree has many uses in addition to the production of fruit. Its trunk is used for timber and to make containers for carrying food and other possessions. The Moroccans use the fronds to construct bulwarks against the advancing sands, lacing them together into a fence about one and a quarter meters high. When a fence is covered by advancing sand, another is built on top. The process is repeated until the dunes reach four and a half meters high and become stable. At that point the dune can be planted with cacti, saltbushes, and wattles, the roots further anchoring the sands place. The grazing lands around the palmeries are now planted with *Atriplex nummular*, an Australian saltbush, which in places has supplanted the native *A. dimorphostegia* and *A. halimus.*

Each palmery consists of land belonging to many different farmers. In places where the traditional agricultural methods are still strong, individual holdings are about eight acres, of which less than twenty-five acres are planted as a traditional palmery, with fruit trees, date palm, seasonal vegetables, and alfalfa. The produce from this small bit of land can provide 60 percent of a household's income. The individual gardens are surrounded by mud brick walls 1.5 to 2 meters tall. These walls act as a deterrent to thieves and animals and as protection on the ground level from the scorching south and the southeast sirocco wind in September and October and the chergui wind from March to May.

Village palmeries are traditionally managed through a complex social organization where the gardens are individually owned but

cooperatively managed. The grove is controlled by a distinguished person, the *amghar n'tamazirt*, who guards the garden. There is another guard, the *amghar n-tiruggin*, for the irrigation system, who is responsible for managing the canals, the reservoirs, and the dams. These guards are chosen by the village elders. The village as a whole is responsible for organizing the opening and closing of the harvest and authorizing the type of weeds that can be cleared along the irrigation canals.

The systems for collection and distribution of water have become important design elements within the gardens. The entire system is carefully regulated, ensuring a appropriate share of the water for each owner. From this communal source, either a spring-fed reservoir or a cistern near the watercourse, water flows through a crisscrossing network of ditches or more elaborate channels to individual holding basins or directly to the trees and crop plots for flood irrigation. This organization creates very rectilinear oasis gardens that tend to resemble one another; the basic structure of these gardens is the same, with individual designs adapted to fit the site and its specific situation.

Recent times have brought other changes in the oasis agricultural system. Because date palm plantations are so lucrative—they can produce as much as six tons of fruit per acre—the majority of these oasis gardens have shifted to palm monocultures, breaking with the old tradition of farming in multiple layers of varying species of dates, fruits, and vegetables. Dwellings have moved outside the arable land, which is today totally devoted to palm cultivation.

A lush, transitional landscape characterizes the lower elevations of the mountains, the edges of the desert, and the banks of the meandering rivers. The landforms of these regions, together with their secluded shady groves and meadows, welcome settlements and villages. Light, filtering through the trees and playing upon the moving grasses and colorful ground cover, defines both the passage of season and the rhythm of place. Each microclimate has its own design, where the rocks, vegetation, and water give scale and shape to forms and delineate the texture of the space.

From their sources among the mountain peaks, rivers hollow out valleys and gorges, forming the lifelines of the country. The riverbanks, adorned with oleanders, are linear oases in a sometimes totally denuded land toward. Poplar, elm, and ash trees dot the banks, marking their paths. In scattered locations, mastic tree (*Pistacia lentiscus*), rockrose, and other native Mediterranean plants grow, adding their texture and color to the riparian fabric.

Bordering villages and towns and within their walls are the "constructed" gardens: productive agricultural plots and orchards, urban gardens, and interior courtyards of buildings and architectural complexes. Productive gardens are found in the plains and uplands of western Morocco, between the Atlas ranges and the Atlantic Ocean, in the intermountain valleys of the Middle Atlas, and in the few oases in eastern Morocco. The farmers have interwoven cultivated and native trees among the small, irregularly

Cultivated fields and a village in the Dadès Valley.

shaped crop fields, building the skeleton of the landscape scenery. The plots contain mostly cereals, including barley, wheat, and maize. These grassy plants cover the land like an ocean, ebbing and flowing in the wind and turning bronze, gold, and green with the seasons. The fields are not only places of work, but also places for social gatherings. Farmers' distant figures are seen throughout the day, their voices carried by the wind over the hills and the valleys to resonate in the canyons. The farmers, both men and women, using mules as the principal draft animals, eke out a living wherever they can find a scrap of productive land.

Almost 80 percent of Morocco's orchards are citrus, primarily oranges, tangerines, and lemons. Figs, almonds, and walnuts are also grown, wherever the soil is suitable and sufficient water is available, and these are an important part of the Moroccan diet. Pomegranates, apricots, peaches, plums, cherries, apples, and pears bear colorful flowers and fruits and are planted in the more temperate climates. Grapes, introduced over the centuries by Phoenician, Roman, and European settlers, are cultivated for both local consumption and export. Olive orchards add a Mediterranean touch to a harsh landscape, with cool gray leaves shimmering in the afternoon sun. The scattered argan forests in the Sous region have a similar feel. Both the olive and the argan are important commercial crops, their fruits used in the production of oils. Flax, cotton, and castor bean are also grown for their oils.

Forests of Mediterranean dwarf palm and esparto grass are found in eastern Morocco, cultivated to provide the farmers with fiber for making paper, ropes, and mats. The plants' ornate shapes are copied and reproduced in tapestries and wall paintings. Other palms, such as the *Washingtonia robusta*, the small Canary palm, and the sabal palmetto, are cultivated in the gardens and urban areas as decorative rather than productive trees.

Most of the aromatic herbs such as coriander, cumin, fennel, sesame, thyme, bay, mint, scented verbena, lavender, and rose are grown, either collectively or individually, often functioning as ground cover in the productive gardens. The prickly pear, brought to Africa from the Americas, is a feature of the landscape, as well as a source of food. It forms a green wall with yellow flowers and fruits, separating one field from another, lining the roads

Mules hauling crops, plowing fields, and threshing grain are common sights in the countryside.

FACING PAGE
*Kasbah Talouet,
Ouarzazate.*

to protect the privacy of landowners, and providing a barrier against straying domestic animals.

In the oases, the traditional irrigation technology of an underground system of deep wells and canals produced an ecosystem that has allowed the Moroccan people to survive for thousands of years. Towns, villages, and farms cluster along the green ribbons of rivers woven through the land. In certain seasons, the intensity of the rivers' flow erodes the fragile soils at the banks. When volume and speed diminish again, the rivers deposit fertile alluvium suitable for intensive cultivation. The damming, canalization, and careful distribution of river water constitute one of the most remarkable feats of Morocco's sustainable system of cultivation.

The harnessing of water has also made possible the variety of constructed urban gardens seen throughout the country. From simple paved courtyards boasting a few potted plants to the luxuriant grand *riyads* of the urban elite, all of Morocco's man-made gardens rely on complex irrigation systems for their survival.

These spaces become of primary importance in Morocco's large cities, images of a natural paradise in the very heart of the most developed areas.

Moroccan wildlife is comprised of both European and African species. The large African game animal that once roamed the land were eradicated during the Roman occupation of North Africa during ancient times. Today, large mammals such as cheetahs (*Acinonyx jubatus*), lions (*Panthera leo*), and panthers (*Panthera pardus*) are threatened. Foxes such as red fox (*Vulpes vulpes*) and fennec fox (*Fennecus zerda*), the wild boar (*Sus scrofa*), the polecat ferret (*Mustela putorius*), jackals (*Canis aureus*), caracals (*Felis caracal*), the small-spotted genet (*Genetta genetta*), and the Egyptian mongoose (*Herpestes ichneumon*) are still present in the southern part of Morocco and in the forests but they are vulnerable to habitat destruction, as are the Barbary sheep (*Ammotragus lervia*) and dorcas gazelle (*Gazella dorcas*). With the help of the government the Barbary macaque (*Macaca sylvanus*) popula-

Crop fields and palmery in the Dadès Valley.

tion is growing in the Atlas region. The Eurasian otter (*Lutra lutra*), harbor porpoise (*Phocoena phocoena*), and various bats and gerbils such as the greater short-tailed gerbil (*Gerbillus maghrebi*) are also considered threatened as a result of habitat destruction and poaching.

The most important wildlife in Morocco is the bird population, nearly five hundred regularly occurring species, of which only thirty-two are endemic. From mosque rooftops to the rivers and marshes, from the High Atlas Mountains to the desert and the oasis, Morocco is an important nesting and resting place for the large variety of migratory birds that make their way between Europe and Africa across the Straits of Gibraltar along the East Atlantic and Black Sea/Mediterranean flyways.

More than 20 million sheep and goats dominate Morocco's cultivated countryside, providing milk, meat, and wool for their herders. These numerous flocks mark the hills with their hoofs and feed on any available plant material. As a consequence of European demand for goat meat, the Berber population of the Atlas Mountains is paid by overseas companies to produce more and more goats, with the larger herds inflicting tremendous damage on the argan tress and coniferous mountain forests.

In addition to domestic goats and sheep, there are more than a million donkeys, along with herds of Mehari and dromedary camels in the south and east, which are used for transport and as draft animals. The slow gait of the dromedary, its peculiar shape, and the tan earth color of its fur are remarkable reflections on the natural elements of its habitat. The animals become elements of the scenery, positioning themselves on the dunes, under the palm trees, or on the *hamada* like domestic cats choosing a location for lounging, trying to attract attention to themselves.

Crops flourish in an alluvial fan at the base of a mountain.

WATER

Water is Morocco's most precious resource. Despite considerable climatic diversity and proximity to the sea, much of Morocco is semiarid or arid. During the winter months, when precipitation does occur, it is variable and unpredictable. Rain and snow feed the headwaters of the rivers and recharge subterranean aquifers, but as the rivers descend toward the valleys and desert, the flow typically slows, the course widens, and water evaporates. In semi-arid zones, soil erosion occurs when the sparse vegetation cannot absorb all of the water that falls on the ground, increasing the possibility of flooding, which further deteriorates the vegetative coverage. In mountainous areas, the pressure of human habitation, combined with unstable geology and intense rainfalls, can easily degrade the soil and render the land uninhabitable.

Alluvial fans spreading out at the foot of the mountain ranges create vast aquifers. These water-bearing strata of rock, sand, or gravel are found even in the extremely arid conditions of the Sahara region. Because aquifers are critical to all facets of life in Morocco, their maintenance is matter of collective concern. Control of water has been a major political and social organizing force in Moroccan society. Large-scale efforts have tended to be most successful in times of peace and stability, when resources are readily available. The availability or scarcity of water has been a determining factor in defining laws and traditions regarding land ownership and inheritance rights. Efforts to manage water resources have in large measure shaped social and political institutions in Morocco, as well as the form of cities and other settlements. Methods of water containment, distribution, and use have also been among the most influential factors in the shaping of Moroccan architecture.

One of the most widespread traditional methods of water catchments and distribution in North Africa and the Middle East is the *qanat* (a Persian term), a system of underground wells that tap into large aquifers. In Morocco, these structures are called *khettara*. The earliest examples of this technology have been traced to Iran and Jerusalem from around 800 B.C. It is theorized that *qanats* originated in Armenia, one of the oldest mining and metallurgical centers in the Near East.

Most of the *khettara* in Morocco are situated on the eastern side of the Atlas ranges. They supply water to oases and settlements in the alluvial foothills at the base of the mountains bordering the Sahara. There are also hundreds of *khettara* located in the Haouz Plain around the city of Marrakech, south of the Tensift River. In Marrakech, the first *khettara* was built during the reign of the Almoravid sharif Ali ben Youssef (1106–1143), under the direction of the engineer Ubayd Allah ibn Yunus, who tapped the aquifer at Akhlij, some forty kilometers from the city. *Khettara* technology was most exploited under the Almohad dynasty, which brought it to other parts of Morocco and to Seville. Over time, the original Moroccan system fell into disrepair; it was eventually restored by the Alawite sharifs in the 1820s.

Changes in the organization of Moroccan society led to a decline in the maintenance of the *khettara* systems, although some of the medium-sized tribal *khettara* have remained in fairly good condition. The largest *khettara* were taken into state ownership in 1925. In the early twentieth century, during the colonial era, the water from both wells and *khettara* was controlled for the benefit of the colonial rulers, a fact that caused hardship and famine for the Moroccan people, especially during the 1930s and the famine of 1945.

In general, *khettara* comprise a series of shafts reaching down to an underground gravity-fed channel. The upper part of the channel, which lies below the water table, serves as an infiltration gallery and may have several branches feeding it. The main body of the channel slopes gradually downhill, delivering water from the aquifer to the cultivated site. Construction and maintenance of *khettara* are not only very labor intensive but also hazardous. Large amounts of earth must be removed, generally using simple hand tools, ropes, and buckets, and workers are hampered by exceedingly cramped quarters. The work of plotting the course of the channel is traditionally the domain of an expert. Siting depends entirely on field experience and the ability to distinguish subtle changes in vegetation that indicate the presence of water. The artisans who construct such systems sometimes travel as a community, migrating from place to place as floods destroy the wells in one area or a lowered water table demands that a tunnel be lengthened in another. In Iran the *qanat* builders are revered and held in high esteem, but in Morocco the lowest classes in the villages have usually been coerced into maintaining the system.

To begin a *khettara*, test shafts are dug to locate the aquifer and assess its depth. After determining the location and permanence of the aquifer, the slope of the site, and the final destination of the water, a series of shafts are dug, thirty to one hundred meters apart. Construction begins at the bottom of the site, with the mother shaft constructed last, at the highest point of the *khettara*. Once the shafts are dug, a long, sloping horizontal channel is dug from the bottom of the lowest shaft toward the mother shaft. The

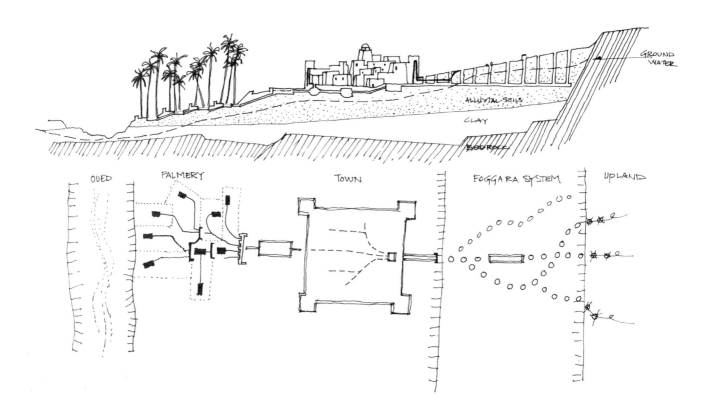

Cross section showing the construction and route of a khettara,
and diagram of the water distribution system.

discharged earth is mounded around the mouth of each shaft to create a raised barrier against storm water. The tunnel is dug on a gradual horizontal slope, so that the water will flow at a fairly slow rate to inhibit erosion. At the mouth of the *khettara*, a large comb-shaped stone (*kesria*) with different-sized openings between the teeth is installed to deliver water according to ownership rights and social status. Water is then carried off by ground irrigation channels (*seguia*) to rectangular holding tanks (*majen*), where it is stored until needed for irrigation.

In towns, *khettara* usually terminate in the marketplace (*souk*), in mosques, or in private homes. *Khettara* passing beneath houses may run through underground rooms and thus function as a cooling device, or be used to fill cisterns and household wells. Complex systems of legal ownership determine the destination of the water and the location of fields, orchards, and residences in relationship to the water source.

Because the demand for water is generally greater than the rate at which the ground water is replenished, the water table is lowered over time. Since the *khettara* utilize water from the highest

point of the water table, when the aquifer is lowered, the *khettara* must be dug deeper. This calls for digging new shafts farther down the slope and moving the mouth of the *khettara* downhill. Irrigated groves and houses must also be reestablished, leaving abandoned orchards and homes at higher elevations where water is no longer available.

Once it is no longer feasible to deepen the *khettara*, a well is dug into the mother tunnel to bring water up to the surface by lift for irrigation. There are still a few examples of traditional lift devices in existence today. The water wheel (*nuria*) used in Fez is similar to the ancient Persian wheel. In the rest of Morocco, *nuria* construction reflects indigenous design. Balanced wells recall the ancient Middle Eastern system of raising water to the surface.

Today, the life of a *khettara* can be extended by pumping water from the main channel out of any of the shafts, regardless of its position on the slope. Pumping costs less in the short run than the labor-intensive maintenance of *khettara* and frees farmers from the restrictions of gravity-fed water systems. The introduction of the diesel pump allowed farming communities, particularly

Water entering the kasbah *from the main* khettara *in the village of Ifran.*   Khettara *directing water through a residential area for household use.*

those of the palm groves, to maintain their locations rather than having to migrate farther down the slope as the water table dropped. The pump thus offers stability to oasis communities, along with an increase in production.

The most important biological water storage systems are the forests, groves, meadows, and orchards. In the more arid zones, oasis trees and specialized ground covers perform the same roles. The fact that plants have the capacity to modify air temperature is only one of their contributions to environmental conditions. Plants also increase the earth's capacity to retain water by activating decomposition and enriching the soil. They also redirect surface water down to natural underground storage areas, making them instrumental in the survival of many animals.

Ground water storage can also be increased through grading and contour modification of absorption beds and channels. Tanks and dams, the most obvious methods of storage, can only be accomplished on a large-scale basis and thus have traditionally been the responsibility of the ruling power in Morocco.

In Morocco's arid and semiarid climate, water runoff must be

Village cistern at the end of the khettara *distribution system.*

Khettara *fallen into disrepair.*

RIGHT
Khettara *outside Ifran. Earthen mounds,*
built with soil excavated during construction,
keep stormwater out of the shafts.

returned to the ground before it can evaporate. Catchment basins, technology developed some four thousand years ago in the Fertile Crescent, allow the harvesting of rainwater and reclamation of irrigation runoff. Catchments are situated below plots of irrigated agricultural land. Small drains on the rocky slopes of the catchment's area direct rainwater to areas of alluvial deposits where water can be stored underground, thereby avoiding evaporation and erosion during times of flooding. The alluvial areas are cleared of large rocks, and small transverse dams, covered with plantings to fight erosion, are constructed with spillways directing water to the alluvial infill.

Conditions in different areas require different water management techniques. On the undulating plains, a simple, low-technology system is used to control runoff. As water flows over the sloping catchment's areas, it is slowed and directed into a basin by a series of small dirt walls surrounding the catchments. At the lowest point of each catchment's area, a tree is planted. The basin is fertilized and the soil is kept loose to increase permeability and

RIGHT
*Ancient channels feed water
to each district in Fez.*

Horizontal waterwheel.

FACING PAGE
A square, vertical nuria, *the
traditional waterwheel of
North Africa.*

*Large waterwheel in Fez, still
used to bring water from a
lower canal into the city.*

maximize runoff storage. The most commonly used trees are olive and almond, since both are deep rooted, drought resistant, and can withstand floods of short duration. In the mountains, where hollows (*rdir*) are formed by wind erosion or the combined forces of water and wind, nomadic tribes enlarge the hollows to trap and store rainwater. Farmers in lower areas build dams along the *wadis* and use a system of dikes to spread the water to the orchards and direct it to storage in special low-level wells. Along the massif of the High Atlas, rock dams are erected, diverting water to small storage tanks. In the desert area of the Great Western Erg, following the course of the Wadi Saoura from Morocco into Algeria, settlements are located in the sand dunes on the left bank at the base of the erg, which provide a natural defensive barrier and climatic protection, as well as a means of storing and filtering water.

Although one of the problems with surface storage in an arid climate is loss through evaporation, large open reservoirs have remained the principal means of water storage in the cities of Morocco. Impressive examples of such works are the water tanks of the Agdal and Menara gardens in Marrakech, the reservoir at the Bou Jeloud garden in Fez, and the Agdal basin in Meknès. Water tanks were usually located in the middle of the garden, surrounded by orchards. The increase in humidity due to evaporation facilitated the growing of trees and crops that otherwise could not tolerate the drying desert wind. Even though the orchard gardens were the property of the *sharifs*, the inhabitants of the city visited them on special occasions, and thus they became public meeting places as well as productive orchards. The water tanks were also said to be used by the military to train soldiers to swim.

Situated in the Taza Pass, in a natural amphitheater at the foot of surrounding hills and at the intersection of two main caravan routes to Algeria and Spain, the city of Fez did not occupy an ideal defensive location. It did, however, have an assured supply of water. At the end of the eighth century, Idriss I, the founder of the city and the first Muslim ruler of the region, purchased the

Low fountain for animals.

FACING PAGE
*One of the one hundred public fountains
scattered throughout Fez.*

rights to local water sources in perpetuity from the local tribes. Under his rule a system of irrigation was established that is still at work today.

The Fez waterworks exemplify a unique and ingenious approach to managing water in a dense urban settlement. The location of the city allowed for the design of a system by which water flowed in channels from the nearby stream through man-made conduits, each serving a different area, before being discharged once again downstream. At the higher reaches of the Wadi Fez, water is first diverted for use in the *agdal* and the royal palaces. In the royal gardens of Bou Jeloud, water is collected and lifted into a series of major channels that flow across the western slope of the city. A channel that branches off from the Bou Jeloud and flows outside the city walls, crossing the Oued Bou Kherareb upstream, supplies the eastern slope. Main conduits feed adjacent properties, the water passing through carved stone screens with openings proportional to the size of the properties. The allotted water is directed by gravity or hoisted up into the residential area by the force of natural pressure into a central basin. Here it passes through another screen to deliver the water to individual households, with the water flowing first into private fountains, then into kitchens, and finally into bathrooms, after which it enters the sewage system. From each dwelling, the sewage merges into progressively larger channels until it merges at the bottom of the valley with the Oued Bou Kherareb, which flows into the Sebou and out to sea.

This flow of water is the determining factor for Fez's organic urban structure; even though the pattern of the water distribution system is concealed under foot, its intricacies are clearly expressed through the urban fabric. Royal palaces are located upstream, the *medersas* are found on the major conduits and springs, while the enclosed orchards and gardens, public fountains, and specific industries (leather tanners and cloth dyers with their mills on steep slopes) are sited according to their traditional economic and social priority and need for fresh running water.

The fountains of Fez are miniature public oases in the city. The Arabic word for fountain, *seqqaya* (plural *aqaqi*), is related to the Egyptian term for a waterwheel and to the word in Farsi meaning "to give drink."

The custom of building fountains fulfils a Koranic injunction to believers to undertake acts of piety and almsgiving. Financing a fountain is such an important civic act that it is not unusual to find an inscription commemorating the founder or the restorer on older fountains. From the writing of Leo Africanus during the sixteenth century, we know that this tradition of fountain building has a long history. He recorded some six hundred fountains in public places, dwellings, and other buildings in Fez in the year 1550. The power of water to sustain life for human and animals, to cleanse and thus protect from disease, and to purify before prayer sanctifies the place in which it is located, whether public street or private dwelling.

The form of the various structures that hold the water is a reflection of the water's dynamics. The canal is water flowing, like the line of an arrow, moving in flight from one place to another. Basins can be either round or rectangular; the rectangular shape speaks of the collection of still water, while the circular form represents the connection between the still and the flowing.

The fountain, being a point of collection and stillness, is usually rectangular. In general, its proportion is usually two units of width to three of height, but there are many variations. The rectangle of the fountain is divided into a basin (*senduq*, often the only part that protrudes from the wall), an upper rectangular border (*toreq*), and a mediating lap, the *hjer*. The *toreq* is surrounded by the *izar*. The fountain is decorated with intricate tile work, and an arch (*dora*) is usually created from tiles to represent the archetypal form of the gate. Since a public fountain is usually located at an important intersection in the quarter, near the mosque or at a *funduq*, the shape of the *dora* and its significance as a gate is doubled. The builders choose a motif for the tile work that will relate the fountain to its particular site.

Public fountains are constructed for the use of both people and animals. Fountains for the specific use of animals are lower to the ground and lack the usual iron grille in front of the *senduq* which is topped with a stone slab, usually eight centimeters thick, sometimes of marble.

The fountain may be as simple as a wall relief or may be an elaborate structure covered with a green tile roof and enclosed by a small portico, turning the entire area into a small point of connection with nature's most precious resource and a gathering place.

Today, the Maghreb is experiencing rapid population growth, with a large percentage of that growth concentrated in urban centers. It is predicted that by the year 2020 water demand will reach the limits of the area's resources. Morocco's rich traditions of survival in a delicately balanced but harsh environment must find ways of adapting to the pressure of the growing population of the modern world.

THE CULTURAL CONTEXT

HISTORICAL INFLUENCES

Archeological findings date prehuman habitation on Morocco's Atlantic coast to as early as 800,000 B.C. By 5,000 B.C., nomadic tribes from the Near East had settled and mixed with the indigenous, sedentary peoples. The Berbers, as these people came to be collectively known, are defined by shared language dialects and culture. Once the majority of the population, Berbers now live in isolated regions of the Atlas Mountains, affiliated by historic tribal connections to their territory and way of life. Their traditional occupations range from those of an agrarian people occupying small towns and villages to nomadic horsemen and shepherds.

By 600 B.C., Phoenician colonists had come to Morocco, bringing with them an ancient system of arboriculture, superb glassmaking craftsmanship, and a textile industry that involved dying linen, cotton, and leather in brilliant hues. They were also expert builders, establishing colonies that eventually grew into cities. Carthage, the largest of these settlements, was founded in 822 B.C. by refugee Phoenician seamen from Tyre. By 300 B.C., their African empire included all the fertile land of the southern Mediterranean coast. This empire lasted until it was conquered by the Romans in 146 B.C.

After the sack of Carthage, the Romans established Tingis (modern Tangier) as the capital of Mauretania Tingitana, their West African colony and accorded it the status of a Roman city. Volubilis became a second capital, followed by a network of towns including Banasa, Salé, Thamusida, Lixus, and Tamuda. The indigenous people, who struggled against the Romans to retain their independence, finally succeeded in freeing themselves in the third century, when the Romans retreated across the Straits of Gibraltar.

Roman civilization had already permeated everyday urban life even before the destruction of Carthage. Africa Romana was based on a colonial agricultural system intended to extract wealth from the land. Roman civilization, however, was essentially urban, centered in towns, and displaying all the characteristic Roman architectural features: forum, basilica, temple, and baths, all richly ornamented with triumphal arches, commemorative columns, statues, altars, tombs, and inscriptions. The Roman influence on Moroccan culture is evident today in the agricultural almanac, which was based on the Julian calendar, and in a majority of agricultural terms that can be traced to Latin roots.

True to the pattern established throughout the empire, the Roman cities of Mauretania Tingitana were supplied with fresh water by well-engineered systems of aqueducts. While most of these have now disappeared, they were used to guide later engineers seeking sources and paths for moving water to new locations. The Romans also introduced the art of ceramic mosaic, which provided the methods and traditions of decoration that inspired the ornamental tile work for which Morocco is famous.

Following the Romans, periods of local rule were intermixed with foreign conquest, the latter including an invasion by the Vandals through Spain and a later Byzantine conquest. Neither succeeded in ruling more than briefly, but they left a legacy in their colorful mosaic work. By A.D. 711, Arab forces had invaded Spain, and Musa ibn Nusayr, the governor of the Islamic province of Ifriquiya (modern Tunisia), had conquered and converted the population of the coastal plains of North Africa. The newly converted Berbers crossed the Straits of Gibraltar to reach the Iberian Peninsula, and within a few years, the caliphs of Damascus controlled all of North Africa and Andalusian Spain.

The era of dynastic rule in Morocco began with Idriss I (reigned 788–791), who called himself Moulay Idriss, and adopted the title "sharif," signaling his claim to princely descent from the prophet Mohammed. Idriss I took refuge in Volubilis, in northern Morocco, where, in 788, he was proclaimed *imam* by the Berber tribes of central Morocco. The position of *imam* implied civil and military leadership as well as religious authority. Idriss I consolidated political power over the northern coastal plateau and mountains. His son (by a Berber concubine) and successor, Idriss II (reigned 803–828), was able to consolidate Idrissid power in the form of a *makhzen*, or central government. Under the Idrissid sharifs, Arabic became the official written language, and the Muslim system of government was established in Morocco. In 808, Idriss II founded the first imperial capital of Morocco at Fez. The city not only became the economic center of northern Morocco, from which Moorish culture emerged, but also developed into an important center of learning and religious thought, influencing the entire Arab world.

Over the next two centuries, tribes from the Arabian Peninsula continued to move in and settle the lower elevations of Morocco. These new immigrants either displaced the Berbers from the more arable land or settled in the cities. They, too, brought with them their own architectural and urban heritage, as well as their crafts and industries, all of which enriched existing forms.

The Idrissid sharifs were eventually replaced by the dynasty of Almoravid sharifs (1056–1147). The dynasty originated in the nomadic tribe of Sunni Berbers of the Sanhaja family, from the High Atlas region southeast of present-day Marrakech. They conquered all of Mauritania as far south as Ghana and eastward into Algiers, uniting Morocco through a theological war. Almoravid sharifs founded a second imperial capital at Marrakech in 1062. Sited at a strategic intersection of important caravan routes, this city is the primary metropolis of southern Morocco. The Almoravids extended their power, establishing a Moslem empire in Andalusia. By 1100, Morocco and all of the Muslim states in

House in the Egyptian style from the period of the New Kingdom (1580–1085 BCE).

Andalusia had come under Almoravid rule, rendering them the major power in the Islamic world.

The Almoravids took with them to Andalusia the traditional form of Berber settlement, an open town surrounded by gardens, palm groves, and orchards of drought-tolerant fruit trees. Water had always been the governing force in the Maghreb; in Iberia, it assumed even more importance. It was tapped, diverted, and displayed in reservoirs, canals, and small rippling fountains decorated with kiln-fired tiles. Walls and shading devices, the main elements for protection from the wind in the desert, took on decorative functions in Andalusia, giving rise to the Moorish garden and courtyard.

In the twelfth and thirteenth centuries, the Almohad dynasts (1130–1269), followers of the conservative Muslim Ibn Tumart, consolidated a Berber Islamic kingdom in Morocco. By 1145, they had succeeded the Almoravid sharifs. The Almohads were responsible for building the kasbah at Marrakech, and they founded a third imperial capital at Ribat al-Fatah (modern Rabat). They took over and completed the cultural policies and projects of the Almoravids, extending and emphasizing the symbiosis between the Andalusian states and the Maghreb region. Almohad sharifs encouraged the cultivation of the arts of music, poetry, and architecture, which under their patronage became firmly established in the cities of Andalusia as well as North Africa, expressing all of the exuberance of the former and the intensity of the latter.

After the fall of the highly urbane and cosmopolitan Almohads, Morocco came under the rule of Berber Merenids, a nomadic people from the deserts of eastern Morocco. Moorish art continued to evolve, influenced by new religious and mystical movements. Sufi mysticism, in particular, became widespread under the Merenid sharifs, infusing the art and crafts of the kingdom with new meanings and symbols. This influence is still seen today in the designs of the *madrasas*, mosques, palaces, and the traditional dwellings they built. Under Merenid rule, the veneration of trees, holy sites, and graves of martyred and honored saints became popular. The Sufi tradition thus revived the ancient concept of *makam* and the tradition of erecting sacred tombs and mausoleums (*mashads*), whose veneration had formerly been widespread throughout Mesopotamia, Phoenicia, and Canaan even before biblical times.

The cultural and political forms that evolved under the sharifan dynasts of Morocco and Andalusia were elaborated through the sixteenth century. With the expulsion of the Moors from Granada in 1492, the last of Spanish Muslims fled to Salé and set up an independent republic that remained intact until 1639. The Portuguese had already left their mark on the North African coast with the founding of fortresses at Ceuta in 1415, Casablanca in 1469, and Asilah and Tangier in 1471. Their influence, confined to a narrow coastal strip, faltered and ended in 1578.

European power began to decline across North Africa at the beginning of the sixteenth century, as interest shifted to exploit-

Remnants of circular basins mark the site of Roman baths in Volubilis.

ing the riches of the New World and Asia, the fierce competition among the new nation states of Europe, and the threat of the rehabilitated Ottoman Empire in the Middle East. Algeria, Tunis, and Libya fell prey to the Ottomans, while Morocco remained under local rule. In 1525, the Beni Saad tribe from the Drâa Valley led a religious war (*jihad*) against the Portuguese on the coast, expelling them from Agadir, Safi, and Essaouira. They gradually gained control of the rest of the country, recapturing Marrakech and later moving north to take Fez. Consolidating their conquests, the Saadian sharifs established an independent state that existed until around 1603. Under their rule, the kingdom of

Riyads *in Fez.*

RIGHT
Kairouine Mosque in Fez.

60

Morocco expanded as far as Timbuktu and the upper bend of the Niger River. Centralized power and wealth generated by caravan trade between central Africa and Europe provided the resources for the restoration of Moroccan cities and the flowering of culture and arts.

After a period of instability, the Saadian dynasts were succeeded by the Alawite sharifs, inhabitants of the Tafilalt oasis. During the 1660s, they had begun with a series of conquests in eastern Morocco, and they eventually succeeded in uniting the rest of the kingdom under their rule. The Alawite dynast Moulay Ismail (1672–1727) consolidated absolute power in the office of the sultancy, eventually driving the Spanish out of Melissa and the English out of Tangier. Moulay Ismail was particularly renowned as a great builder who envisioned Meknès as a fourth imperial capital of Morocco. To that end, he enlarged the old town, constructed an immense palace, and built a series of granaries. He also built a garden complex spanning ten acres south of the city, with a reservoir fed by a fifteen-mile-long system of conduits. With the help of European engineers and Christian slave labor, he enlarged the town of Mogador-Essaouira into an important port city. Ismail's reign marked the end of the independent Moroccan kingdom. Throughout the nineteenth century, the country was plagued by unrest and civil war, and the European powers once again began to exercise their interests in North Africa.

Following negotiations among rival European powers, culminating in the Treaty of Fez in 1912, France gained control of Morocco. The institutions of the sultancy and the *makhzen* were preserved with the Alawite sharifs remaining in power. Rabat became the base of the French governors, expanding with the influx French colonists who were both able and willing to exploit the economic base of the country. Today the city is the administrative capital of Morocco. Modern European enclaves and their corollary "native" shantytowns dominated the urban landscape of Morocco in the colonial period. To strengthen their control, the French built a network of roads, railways, and power plants and introduced new crops and agricultural techniques.

In the 1930s, Islamic students and faculty from the University of Fez, together with the first generation of a Western-educated elite, began organizing an independence movement. Their demands were outlined in the 1944 Manifesto of Independence. During the course of World War II, Sultan Mohammed V's sympathy for the nationalist movement had steadily grown. By 1953, the struggle for independence against the French forced his abdication and exile. Splintered resistance groups and the rural populace, who were offended at the insult to their religious leader, pledged their loyalty to the sultan, leading to more and more frequent acts of defiance. Facing open rebellion by the mountain tribes and violent rebellion throughout North Africa and Asia, France was forced to sign the French–Moroccan Agreement on March 3, 1956, granting the country full independence.

Following independence, Mohammed V took steps to create a

Buildings in Meknès constructed partly with materials looted from the surrounding cities of Volubilis and Marrakech.

FACING PAGE
Hill town of Chechaouene. The blue and white color of the houses reveals the influence of Andalusian refugees who settled the site.

modern Islamic state. He drew up a constitution and held elections, attempting to industrialize the country under a joint system of monarchy and parliamentary control. His son, Hassan II, succeeded to the throne in 1961 and was, in turn, succeeded in 1999 by his son, Mohammed VI, the current monarch.

Even as it embraces the global community, Morocco has also worked to preserve its unique cultural heritage. With the help of its modern rulers, who have worked to reestablish the craft industries and revitalize cultural institutions, the living traditions of Moroccan art forms, the product of long centuries of vibrant transculturation, continue to thrive throughout the country, from the rural settlements of the valleys and desert oases to the elegant homes of European expatriates and the Moroccan elite.

Traditonal geometry of medersas
*and minarets in Fez. Green tiles
symbolize Islam, and the minaret
is topped with a* Jamour *ornament.*

BUILDING
ELEMENTS

Building forms in Morocco embody deep religious meanings and function as a system of social communication and interaction. Architecture has become one of the formal languages through which the Islamic experience has been transmitted from place to place, from one generation to another. The act of constructing buildings and settlements has helped Islam's devotees to understand their religious experience as they use their designs to express and reinterpret their own beliefs.

Morocco's location on the African continent, its indigenous Berber culture, the impact of Middle Eastern culture and Roman civilization, the influence of nomadic Bedouin conquerors from the Arabian peninsula and the Mediterranean cultures of Europe have produced a unique architectural tradition. This synergetic heritage produced refined and elaborate structures that were carried to Spain by the Muslim sharifs who ruled there. Through this fusion of Moroccan and Spanish forms, Moorish architecture was born. It was eventually returned to the Maghreb, where craftsmen and designers continue to deploy its traditions today.

The architects of Moroccan buildings use a basic repertoire of elements. The scale of structures and rooms and the significant detailing of interior elevations reflect religious rituals and cultural practices. Light is used to connect and transform open and enclosed spaces and becomes a powerful means of distinguishing between public and private domains. The formal vocabulary common to all types of structures includes elements such as pointed or scalloped horseshoe arches, ribbed or stalactite vaults, and ornament such as tracery, carved stucco, calligraphic inscription, and mosaic tile. These elements reflect the close connections among all of the architectural traditions that have been introduced into Morocco and those discovered in conquered lands such as Andalusia. Specific meanings of both ancient and modern architecture can only be understood in the light of religious beliefs and practices.

The traditional buildings of Morocco were made of pounded earth faced with stucco or mud, two very ancient techniques common in Africa. To make pounded earth, wet soil is mixed with straw or gravel, with lime added for increased durability. Gravel or stone is sometimes added instead of the more expensive lime. Mud and baked bricks, also faced with stucco, came into use after the capture of Spain for the construction of walls built on rubble foundations. Wood is scarce and is used sparingly throughout North Africa, primarily for the decoration and articulation of structural members. Stucco is heavily employed for interior decoration, an integral part of every Moroccan building.

No Moroccan city would be complete without its *bab*, or arched gate. Surviving remains of triumphal arches installed under Roman rule in North Africa may have inspired the first such gates, but the Moroccans carried the form to a high level of sophistication. The central horseshoe arch is common to these city gates, but semicircular arches set in the wall are also frequently seen. The latter form refers to the Islamic notion of "squaring the circle," reflecting the dual roles of heaven and earth. In Morocco, city gates are typically ornamented with the trappings of fortified architecture, such as stepped merlons, but they also exhibit calligraphic decoration and subtle features, such as obliquely set bricks. The common Islamic lozenge tracery is often

LEFT
Ruined royal stables of Moulay Ismail, which once held as many as 12,000 horses.

FACING PAGE
Granary, Meknès.

House in the High Atlas Mountains constructed of local stone and sun-baked loam bricks. The flat roof is made of beams overlaid with small branches and twigs, then covered with a thick layer of pounded earth.

RIGHT
Pisé (rammed earth) houses, Tin. Dwellings are built on the hillside to reserve the fields for agriculture.

used for decoration, creating a play of light and shadow over the gate. The most elaborate example of such gates is the Bab Mansour in Meknès, which was completed in the eighteenth century.

The old center (*medina*) of Moroccan cities is the focus of urban society, where religion is woven into every aspect of life. Moroccan towns are often divided into quarters, which are typically differentiated by activities and occupations of their inhabitants. Focused on daily work and exchanging goods in the marketplace, residents live in close proximity to one another and to their shared institutions. Houses are crowded together, forming a labyrinthine network of walkways. Oriented inward toward courtyards and gardens, the architecture of the *medina* does not

City gate, Meknès.

LEFT
Chellah necropolis gate, Rabat.

FACING PAGE
*Merinid period minaret of the Cherabliyn
Mosque, Fez, showing traditional delicate white
lozenge tracery over a pale green ceramic base.*

*Tile and carved wood decoration on a wall sur-
rounding the Ben Youssef Medersa, Marrakech.*

Roofs of the sanctuary of Moulay Idris, Fez.

reveal itself to passersby. The severe facades of the dwellings do not distinguish between rich and poor. Even the splendor of the mosque is not evident on the exterior. Thick walls shelter family and spiritual life from the din of the street.

Since the middle of the ninth century, the central building of every Moroccan city has been the mosque, the physical manifestation of religious and secular power. In Morocco, mosques are typically hypostyle structures with a single minaret and an elaborate niche (*mihrab*) oriented toward Mecca for prayer. The form of Moroccan mosques can be traced to examples from seventh- and eighth-century Iraq. This form was transplanted to newly conquered territories, perhaps to provide a flexible space for public prayer that could be tailored to the size of different congregations.

The second most important building in the Moroccan city is the *medersa*, a complex that functions as a theological school or seminary and can double as a congregational mosque as well. The establishment of a *medersa* is subject to strictly applied conventions. The patron family or benefactors relinquish their rights to the property, which is given to the state as a religious endowment (*hubus*). The donated property is exempt from taxes, and all proceeds support institutional activities and scholarships for stu-

dents. *Medersa* plans exhibit the typical Moroccan architectural idioms, which divide and subdivide spaces in seemingly endless progression. The *medersa* has traditionally been the center of culture where learned persons (*ulamas*) congregated. *Ulamas* still preside over the education of young and old and wield political influence over secular rulers.

The rural counterpart of the *medersa* is the *zawiya*, which developed around the fifteenth century. The *zawiya* denotes the location of a holy man's grave or place of residence. The area becomes a shrine with the construction of a mausoleum. In the case of the tomb of Idriss I, for example, the entire area became a pilgrimage center. In addition to the mausoleum, the *zawiya* complex consists of a prayer room, usually modest in size, individual cells to accommodate pilgrims seeking blessing (*baraka*), and a residence for the administrator of the site, who collects gifts and alms and ministers to pilgrims and visitors. In some instances, there will be a cemetery for followers of a particular holy man.

One of the important secular structures in Moroccan towns is the *funduq*. These buildings originated as lodging houses to accommodate travelers, much like the fortified caravansary constructed along trade routes to accommodate merchants and

FACING PAGE AND LEFT
*Najjarin Funduq, Fez. Goods are
sold from the facade facing the street.*

pilgrims in Iran and other parts of the Islamic world. Shops and warehouses traditionally occupy the lower floor fronting the street. Animals were housed in the central interior courtyard, which functioned as a stable. As in the medersa, the upper level has covered galleries leading to the bedrooms for visitors. Today, *funduqs* are used mainly for warehousing merchandise, but their architecture generally remains unchanged.

Traditional houses (*dar*) in towns and rural communities of Morocco resemble Roman courtyard dwellings. They are typically two to three stories high with pitched roofs facing inward, with the rooms clustering around an interior courtyard that may or may not be open to the sky. The door marking the main entrance is ornately designed with metal studs, hinges, and painted deco-

ration. Metal and wood are integral to Moroccan buildings, incorporated in lighting fixtures, furniture, doors, window details, grilles, and ornate balconies. On the interior, houses are tranquil and spacious. Cushions, mats, carpets, and serving tables are put away when not in use to maintain the openness of the space.

Unique to Moroccan architecture are the Berber citadels (*agadir* or *tighremt*), found in such diverse areas as the High Atlas and the Drâa Valley. Reminiscent of towers in ancient Sumerian towns, they can be as small as granaries or large enough to shelter an entire village.

The *tighremt* is a specific type of fortified dwelling three stories high, with the lower level serving as an enclosure for farm animals, the second level as a granary, and the third level as living

Decorative patterns etched into the loam walls of a tighremt.

LEFT
A tighremt, *or square Berber fort.*

quarters. The *ksar* (the dwelling place of a local ruler) and the
kasbah (the fortified village) are often similar in appearance; each
compound is designed to house several families behind high
walls. Towers, located at the corners or at the entrance, serve as
storehouses, and a covered well is typically located within the
fortress walls.

In the rural areas of Morocco, the characteristic building material is loam. The *ksar* and the *tighremt* are the most notable examples of the beauty and versatility of this material. Loam
housing is either made from stacked, unbaked bricks or in a similar technique to rammed earth. A slush of clay plaster veneers the
loam to maintain its durability. In the urban settlements, baked
clay brick is the common construction material. Both clay and
loam are used for interior and exterior flooring. The hard exterior
flooring is called *desks.** Similar material is used for outer wall
(*medluk*). It consists of a mixture of sandy loam spread with lime
slush and pounded for several hours. After it hardens, it is polished
further by hand using a rough stone. Some people use a finish of
raw egg, which hardens to a shine and can be maintained easily.
The material creates a plain, hard surface that acts as a foil for the
ornate facade decorations on the exterior and interior elevations.

Stone is a scarce and highly prized building material. Rose soft
stone from Salé is employed in some buildings, mainly for wall
decorations, columns, capitals, pedestals, and some facade
cladding. Marble is especially used in the mosques, the medersas,
and other public buildings. Found in quarries near the major
cities, marble ranges in color from black and gray to light beige
and even dark pink. White or white with several interesting veins
are prized for columns and flooring. Despite its hardness, it is
also intricately carved as window and partitions. The smoothness
of the marble makes it suitable for fountain design, with the material allowing the water to reflect and attract light. Morocco has
exported marble to Europe since Roman times. It was known all
over the Islamic world and is still sought after today.

Decorative carving. Chellah necropolis, Rabat.

RIGHT
Hexagonal columns of soft rose stone from Bouknadel, valued for its warm color. El Badi Palace, Marrakech.

MATERIALS AND DECORATION

Moroccan architectural forms are minimalist, and a strict dichotomy is maintained between public and private worlds. Behind the plain exterior are interior spaces with lavish courtyards and rooms with richly ornamented surfaces, tiled or decorated with stucco or bands of calligraphy, all of which enrich and balance the traditional austerity of the architectural forms.

Within Moroccan buildings, the concept of the void is exemplified only in spatial terms. Every inch of surface—walls, vaults, ceilings and floors—will be embellished in some manner. The decoration and the articulation of these surfaces are based on complex geometric orders. Using infinite repetitions and combinations of patterns, designers break the division of the structural forms and create an illusion of transitions between the structural zones, such as the area between a dome and its square base or between wall and ceiling. In the garden, the delineation of zones is achieved by multiplying the pattern or by minute changes of elevation. The space and the pattern complement each other, drawing the viewer's attention and encouraging contemplation of the infinite.

All Moroccan craftsmen work within the same basic decorative system. No matter what material is being used, the decoration will follow one or more established styles. *Tastir* is created from straight-sided geometric elements. Basic shapes include the square, equilateral triangle, circle, spiral, and pentagon. The artist places these shapes on a grid (either square or isometric), then creates his design by drawing lines between the points of intersection. The pattern repeats off into infinity, only interrupted by the frame of the next architectural element. *Tastir* patterns are commonly based on the octagon (*muthamman*), hexagon (*musad-*

das), twenty-pointed star (*'ishrini*), twenty-four-pointed star (*ar-ba'wa 'ishrini*), fifty-pointed star (*khamsini*), and herringbone (*damluji**). *Tawriq* designs are made up of leaf and floral shapes. *Tawriq* designs are generally much more fluid than the *tastir*, although the geometries are carefully considered in this style as well. Tashjir designs consist of tree motifs. The elaborate shapes of the intertwining boughs, leaves, and fruits are usually rendered in polychrome paint on wood panels.

It is traditional to incorporate a verse from the Koran or a saying of the Prophet into a design. The stylized letters may be rendered in the squared *kufic* hand, or in the rounded cursive *naskhi* style. Calligraphy can be integrated within larger designs or, more commonly, used to create a frieze above the *zellij* (mosaic tile) panels on the lower part of the walls. This band will often run around an entire room, encircling the space with a poem or religious inspiration. Some artists use an abstraction of the *kufic* script to create decorative lines with the square feeling of the calligraphy, but without any meaning attached. These *kufic* lines are used to produce beautiful borders and plaits within larger designs. Because no space can be left empty, a pattern of small regular motifs may be used to cover areas between larger designs. Honeycomb patterns are often used to provide a neutral fill within more elaborate decorations.

Moroccan craftsmen work with a variety of materials, including wood, metal, earth, stone, brick, and plaster. Each has the power to express a different facet of the traditional design motifs. Geometric shapes carved into white plaster are hypnotic, a pure meditation on the infinite; when the same pattern is rendered in polychrome tile, it becomes as lively and colorful as

a flower garden. Painted tashjir decorations on a wooden panel have a lighthearted quality; the same flowers and vines executed in metal filigree are more sophisticated and elegant. By varying the material, the designer can produce a variety of effects from these design motifs.

Timber is more available in Morocco than in other North African countries because of the dense forests in the Middle Atlas region. The fragrant Atlas cedar (*ilerz*) has traditionally been the most commonly used architectural wood; it is worked after it has dried, and a properly cured piece does not need to be treated or varnished. Cedar is fashioned into a variety of decorative and structural elements, including screens, doors, lintels, windows, ceilings, and balustrades. Berber thuya, argan, and *wiwani* are also used. Ebony imported from Madagascar and mahoganies from the Ivory Coast and Gabon are sometimes worked into special decorative details.

The popular belief is that the first wood master was Noah, builder of the Ark, who bestowed his talent and his knowledge on the woodcarver families of Morocco. Woodwork is done only by men organized in guilds, where the membership is often hereditary and the techniques are passed from father to son. Projects are designed and executed in the master's workshop and brought to the site for installation.

Wood is used in architectural details, incorporating calligraphy and the arabesque floral and geometric patterns found in all other artifacts. These designs can be carved, painted, turned, or inlaid, according to the effect the craftsmen wish to produce. Intricate geometric shapes are carved in small pieces and assembled in the same manner as the *zellij* tiles. Fluid *tawriq* motifs are first cut into a stencil then transferred to the wood for carving.

Painted wood panels (*zwaqs*) are decorated with brightly colored botanical motifs or geometric designs and sealed with a light coat of varnish. Examples of the most elaborate work in wood are *muqarnas* (pieces of wood descending like stalactites from a vaulted ceiling) and the *moucharabia* (turned wooden screens) installed in the upper gallery or on the outer wall of the houses to allow for ventilation and conceal women observing activities in the courtyard below.

Bronze, brass, and copper are ubiquitous in household objects and utensils and are also used in architectural decorations such as "good luck" Fatima hands, lamps, chandeliers, door knockers, bolts, hinges, and rooftop spires (*jamour*). Monumental doors of carved and studded brass are used for important buildings such as mosques and royal palaces. In contrast, ironwork decoration is very limited. Wrought iron is only found in window grilles and door decorations such as nails, hinges, and knockers. Grilles are worked into spiral and foliated designs and rarely follow the articulated geometric shapes used in other crafts. The Moroccan ironwork tradition is the result of Spanish influence and is principally found in the coastal cities once occupied by the Spanish. Iron is still considered a material for the poorer classes and is little valued as decoration.

In other parts of the world, plaster (*gyps*) decorations are molded in a production facility, transferred to the site after hardening, and then installed in place. In Morocco, plaster decorations are carved in place. Workmen smooth the soft Moroccan plaster onto walls and ceilings to a depth of several centimeters. The composition of the plaster allows it to harden slowly, allowing time for the intricate carving. The design can be modified by dampening the surface and reworking the plaster. Even though

Entrance doors to palaces and other richly appointed buildings are often carved and worked into elaborate designs.

plaster can be used to cover large surfaces, it is never prepared in large quantities. Instead it is mixed carefully by hand in small pans to create the required texture and produce the subtle inconsistency that gives the material its flexibility and fluidity. The pattern is transferred to the panel with a stencil; the most experienced masters use just ruler and dividers. The pattern is repeated many times across the surface to create the desired rhythm. The finished plaster design may be highlighted in paints of various color or covered with whitewash.

Plaster is usually used for upper walls, for the transitional area between two materials such as *zellij* and wood carving, or as a bridge between structural elements such as the upper wall and ceiling. The flowing imaginative designs, especially the calligraphic forms, provide direct contrast to the strict angularity and geometry of the *zellij* tile work on the lower parts of the room.

The height of plaster craftsmanship is the design of special decorative elements. Like the wooden stalactite decorations after

which they are modeled, plaster *muqarnas* provide three-dimensional fill for vaulted areas and niche ceilings. The other specialized plaster decoration is the *chemmassia*, a plaster stained glass window panel. *Chemmassiat* are not carved in place. A wooden form is filled with plaster; when dry, it is carved deeply, creating small openings within the design. Colored glass is pressed into the openings, and the finished panel is installed in its niche, usually high on a wall. These window panels soften the harsh Moroccan sunlight, illuminating interiors and providing colorful highlights against the delicately tinted plaster shapes.

Perhaps the most typically Moroccan decorative material is *zellij*, the brightly colored tile mosaics. *Zellij* is an integral part of a building and is planned for from the initial stage of the design. Like other surface materials, *zellij* functions as more than mere embellishment. This multidimensional art form has deep religious meanings expressed through its geometries and the mathematic and astrological significance the figures carry. They hypnotic, repetitive designs are used to foster a meditative and religious connection to the Divine.

Zellij are small glazed clay tiles of different shapes that are assembled into geometric, calligraphic, and floral designs and then mortared into place. This craft has thrived as a continuous living traditional art form since the Phoenicians arrived on the North African coast, bringing with them the art of ceramic mosaic from its originators (the art is variously credited to the Greeks, the Romans, and the Syrians). Ruins at Volubilis and Lixus exhibit fine examples of Roman mosaic work, which was applied in private and public spaces, on interior and exterior elevations, and in the patterns of floors. Some of the earliest examples of *zellij* are found on the Almohad minarets of the mosques at Kutubiyya and the kasbah at Marrakech. Fine examples of *zellij* from the period of the dynasty of al-Ahmar can be found in Seville, Granada, Córdoba, Málaga, and Toledo. The most notable examples can be seen at the Alhambra Palace in Granada.

Spanish-influenced ceramics retained many traditional designs, but large tiles (*azulejos*) replaced the small ones, and patterns were painted on them to speed production. In the fifteenth century, the Muslims and Jews who had been expelled from Spain and immigrated to Morocco contributed to the further enrichment of the *zellij* tradition, creating a derivative painted polychrome tile influenced by the more florid *azulejos*.

Historically the two most important centers of production have been Fez and later Tetouan. While Fez was the earliest of the imperial capitals, established by Idrissid dynasts in 808, Tetouan was a relatively new town, established between 1484 and 1485 by Muslims of the Nasrid kingdom of Granada. Because of its position on the Mediterranean coast near Tangier, Tetouan became a focal point of cultural confluence for Berber and Andalusian arts. Distinctly different methods of producing *zellij* were developed at Fez and Tetouan, each taking a specific approach to the process of determining the final shape of the individual tile

*Large pieces of wood are often reserved
for decorative purposes.*

FOLLOWING PAGES
Courtyard of the Dar Batha Museum in Fez.

(*furmah*), as well as to the mode of assembly of the finished panel.

Since the Middle Ages, Fez has been the most important city in the production of *zellij*. Fez was the capital and a cultural center during the Merenid period when the art of *zellij* flowered in Morocco. It was home to the Kairouine University, a center of trade and the hub of a rich agricultural region. *Zellij* found in other towns such as Meknès, Marrakech, Rabat, and Salé was either imported from Fez or was produced in the Fassi tradition of sophisticated and complex designs.

In the past, *zellij* production was controlled by guilds and dominated by a few powerful families whose function it was to consult with the architect and builders in the design of a project from the beginning of the process through its realization, maintaining a standard of quality in all detail work to ensure the distinctive Fassi style. To halt the decline of the craft that was occurring in the mid-twentieth century, Fez established a potters' cooperative and the Fez Zellij Cooperative in the 1960s. The cooperative system has been very successful in securing work on both a national and international scale. *Zellij* in modern Fez has become an important industry in response to the demand of the building trades.

Traditional Tetouan *zellij* is very plain. In the sixteenth and seventeenth centuries, patterns were limited to checkerboard and simple rectilinear designs. The Morisco immigrants who settled in Tetouan seem to have been influenced by the austere provincial Mudejar architectural styles, not by ornate Andalusian palaces. The early eighteenth-century *zellij* of Tetouan and neighboring Tangier tended to remain plain and limited in application, with the exception of works commissioned by the governor Basha Ahmad al-Rifi between 1713 and 1743 for the Mashwar Palace of Tetouan and the Tangier kasbah.

TOP
*Green and white zellij tilework floor.
Hotel Mamounia, Marrakech.*

ABOVE
*Green and tan tile borders enliven
a concrete floor. Palais Jamaï, Fez.*

RIGHT
*Wooden ceiling painted with delicate floral
designs. Hotel Mamounia, Marrakech.*

Today, Tetouan *zellij* makers remain conservative, using traditional methods to produce their tiles. Clay is first cleaned and soaked in indoor basins, then wedged and worked into a brick, which is further shaped into a slab of precise thickness. The raw clay is cut with wooden dies to the shape of the finished tile. After drying to leather-like consistency, the *furmah* is given a final trimming and a first firing. The tile is then dipped in glaze and fired for the second and final time. Tiles may be made in differing thickness according to their function. When the tile is completed, it is delivered to the craftsman who will install the work.

The Tetouan technique of individually working each tile does not lend itself to modern manufacturing methods. The process is slow, and the work is produced and supervised by a single master in a single workshop. In Tetouan, each job is supervised by just two master craftsmen—one in whose workshop the *furmab* are made, and one who executes the design.

The Tetouan National School of Arts and Crafts was founded in 1926 to preserve the city's traditional craft. It offers a seven-year course in *zellij* that includes plane and spherical geometry, calligraphy, drawing, traditional patterns, and studio art and covers the handling of materials and observation of all phases of *zellij* making, including the execution of sample projects.

Historically, the earnings of the potter were considered pure because they derived from the earth with which God created mankind. In accordance with his status, the traditional *zellij* artisan must devote his life to his art. *Zellij* represents the homage of the artist to the simplicity of the material from which man derives, in contrast to the infinite complexity of the universe. The

Star-shaped tiles in the courtyard.
Hotel Mamounia, Marrakech.

FACING PAGE
The Najjarin fountain in front of the
funduq *opposite the Kairouine Mosque.*

Carved wood, carved plaster and zellij.
Ben Youssef Medersa, Marrakech.

study and memorization of the Koran constitutes both the artisan's body of knowledge and the inspiration for his work. Designs are based on a numerological system originating with the four cardinal directions and the infinite variations and patterns emanating from them. Layers of patterns emerge, repeating and embellishing simple geometric forms and mirroring the profound nature of the cosmos. "God is beautiful and loves beauty," affirms the Prophet Muhammad, as was told in the Hadith.

Traditional Moroccan *zellij* used turquoise and white monochrome tiles embedded in mortar and fastened with nails to wooden facings to produce larger-scale mosaic friezes and moldings. Later the palette expanded to include seven colors—three basic (white, black, and sandalwood brown) and four complementary (red, green, yellow, and blue). This seven-color system is used throughout the Islamic world and is based on the sacred associations of the numbers three, four, and seven. Designs will use either two contrasting colors (especially white with blue or green) or will mix all the colors in a polychromatic composition. Most *zellij* designs are geometric, but calligraphic designs, depicting verses from the Koran and poetry, and stylized floral designs are also common.

In interiors, *zellij* is used in combination with intricately carved plaster and wood. The white or beige plaster is carved in stalactite-like forms, usually above a doorway or arch, and in floral and plant motifs on intricate panels above revetments. Wooden wall panels and ceilings are dark with painted designs in blues, greens, reds, and gold; the designs can be especially ornate on portals.

Zellij has been used most intensively in interior courtyards, where floors, walls, fountains, pillars, and stair risers are tiled. Other such interior applications have been found in the *medersas* and in the prayer and reception halls of mosques. In outdoor spaces, *zellij* is used to highlight focal points such as fountains, benches, gates, and entrances to public spaces and monuments, where the polychrome mosaics offer a durable, easy-to-maintain protective surface. The multicolored tiles form rich designs that contrast with the neutral and warm shades of plaster and stone. Epigraphic tiles confer blessings on the owner of the property, quote poetry and religious verses, and refer to the paradise of heaven recreated on earth. The most common design is a circle of colored squares surrounded by black in repeated form. Alternating between dark (green, blue, and black) and light (white or yellow) squares is very typical. In the house Bands of *zellij* accentuate changes in elevations, the transition between horizontal and vertical surfaces, and the edges of fountains. The columns and the lower part of the walls are sometimes covered with *zellij* panels. Panels are used on the floors, at the entrances and in the middle of the rooms resembling carpets. Because climate and the play of light are major factors in the design of urban spaces and individual buildings, colors are determined by the light levels where the *zellij* panel is to be located.

The renaissance of *zellij* came with the rise of the national independence movement under the reigns of Mohammed V and Hassan II. Realizing that only a handful of skilled *zellij* craftsmen remained, King Hassan II, known as "the Builder," established schools for the conservation and rejuvenation of this art. The king supported his effort by requiring *zellij* to be used in every public building constructed by the state. This dictum had the effect of stimulating the production of new colors and designs and, eventually, a unique style called "Hassani." Hassani *zellij* has had a great influence on modern Islamic and Islamic-influenced architecture throughout the world.

Although *zellij* has had a modern renaissance, some believe that today's demands for speed and economy have led to a lowering of the standards of the past. Some modern builders influenced by international styles tend to see *zellij* as decoration rather than an integral part of the initial design, not taking into account the ancient conventions of proportion, scale, and color. However, there is a strong movement in contemporary Moroccan architecture to successfully integrate the two.

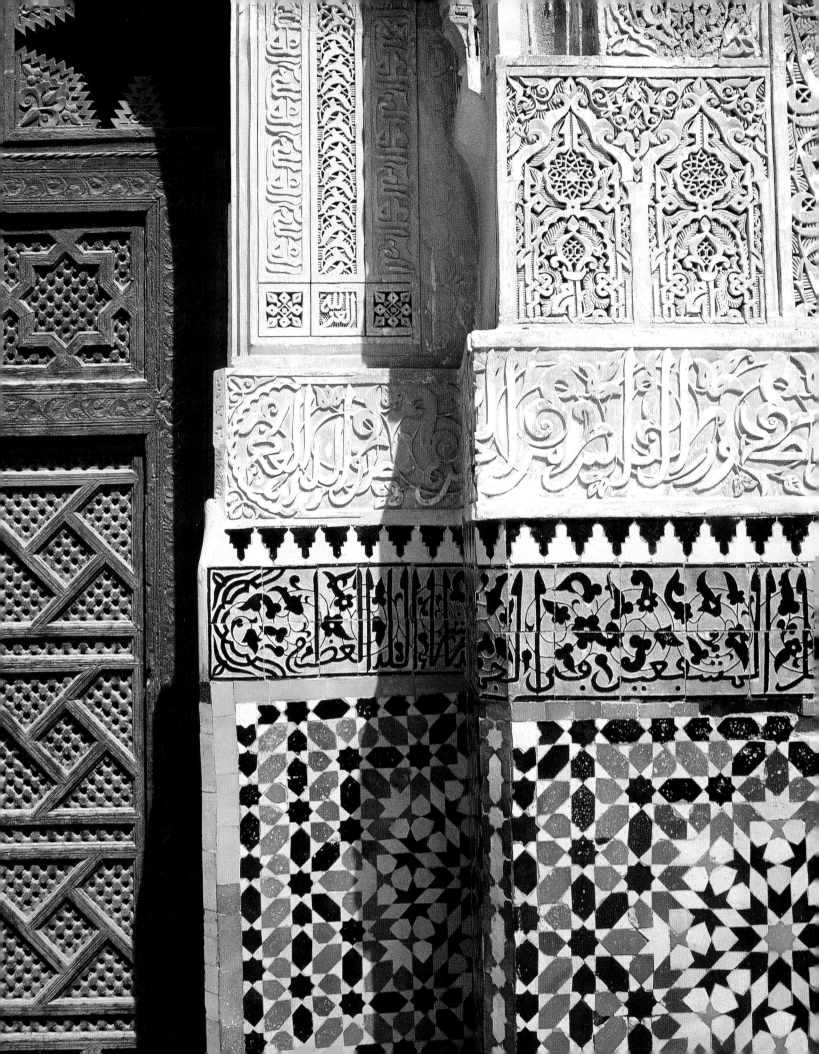

COURTYARDS
AND GARDENS

THE *DAR* AND THE COURTYARD

The Moroccan courtyard is an essential element of the basic urban dwelling: the *dar*. The house is the most precious possession of the individual and represents his status in the material world. The tradition of the *dar* dates back thousands of years. Some contend that the form stems from that of the ancient houses of Mesopotamia, Greece, and Rome; others (such as Jean Gallotti) consider the main influence to be the organization of the traditional Moroccan nomadic camps.

Typically, the traditional *dar* comprises one or more two- or three-story structures surrounding an open rectilinear courtyard. Two salons are located on the first floor in addition to a special reception room for entertaining guests, a kitchen and a washroom. All the first-floor rooms open directly onto the courtyard, while those on the upper floors open onto an arcaded gallery or balcony. The rooms are typically about 2.75 to 3 meters wide, 6 to 14 meters long, and 4.5 meters high, their dimensions constrained by the length of the wood available for rafters. In addition to living rooms and bedrooms, the upper floors usually house a second cooking area and utility washroom. This may be used only during the winter when the family lives upstairs or every day if an extended family shares the house, with some living downstairs and some on the upper floors. Low-ceilinged storage rooms for grain, olives, and oil are located between the two floors.

One or two narrow staircases lead to the upper rooms, separating the public space from the private domain. The roof has a terrace and occasionally boasts a large reception room, the most beautiful room in the house, reserved for special guests. This rooftop pavilion will be ornately decorated and painted, and the windows will offer a panoramic view of the *medina* or the surrounding landscape.

The *dar* typically presents a very plain face to the street. There is no ornamentation on the street facade and no overt distinction between the homes of the wealthy and the other residents. The houses usually connect directly to the adjacent buildings on three sides, with the fourth side on the street. Urban dwellers sometimes expand their *dars* over the alleys and streets by bridging the top floors and adding more rooms. The street facade usually has a large single or double front door with smaller doors set inside the monumental frame for daily use. Narrow openings allow views of the public life on the street. The doors are decorated with two iron door-knockers, one higher for use by horseback riders and one lower for visitors on foot. Other decorations can include a stylized hand of Fatima for good luck or linear or geometric design worked in large nails.

The outdoor province of the women comprises the courtyard and the open roof terrace at the top of the house, unless male guests are using those spaces. The roof is sometimes adorned with a parapet or walls to screen the female inhabitants while they go about their domestic chores. Family groups—exclusively male or female—gather on the roof at night to sit, socialize, and even to sleep under the open sky in hot weather.

Only prosperous families have the resources to build and maintain a *dar* or other home in the center of the *medina*. Most of the poorer families live at the outskirts of the cities or outside the city walls in very modest dwellings based on similar design ideas but at a much more limited scale.

Other dwellings in Morocco include the *dwira*, a small house with a small paved courtyard and one room upstairs and one

LEFT
A passageway between two houses on a main street provides a semi-private meeting space.

FACING PAGE
In an unplanted patio courtyard, or ouest ed-dar, colorful tiles and the fountain add interest to the space, and surrounding green roofs evoke the tops of trees peering over the walls. Moulay Ismail Palace, Rabat.

Planted riyads *add touches of green to the Marrakech skyline.*

eos*Roman capitals juxtaposed with Islamic decorative elements. Museum of Moroccan Arts, Tangier.*

down and the *massreiya,* a small guest house attached to a larger house. Its top floor has a salon and the ground floor is used as a shop, for storage, or for animals. It is used by male guests or by the eldest son and his friends.

The heart of every *dar*—whether dwelling, religious institution, or commercial building—is the open interior space. This area takes into consideration the three basic human needs: provision for bodily comfort, satisfaction for the individual soul and spirit, and intellectual preoccupation with cultural ideals and concepts.

Since the main doors of each room open onto the central courtyard or the balcony, it is the principal circulation space in the *dar.* Light, sound, colorful decoration, and comfortable temperatures combine to make the courtyard the focus of the house. It marks the transition from the public domain to the tranquility and refuge of the private arena. The noise and dust of the street are left outside; inside it is quiet and cool, sheltered from the desert heat and the bustle of the public world.

This interior space plays an important role in creating a more moderate climate within the entire dwelling. Breeze in the summer and warmth at night and in the winter are of prime impor-

tance in making the desert hospitable to human habitation. Low, wide courtyards can capture cooling breezes, while taller buildings provide more shade and shelter from the hot sun. In the summer, the shaded recesses of the patio and cool tile floor provide additional relief from the heat. In winter and during cool summer nights, the tiled floors absorb heat during the day and transfer it to the rest of the house.

Ventilation through the courtyard also helps to mediate the indoor climate of the *dar.* The doors to the patio let light and air into the adjoining rooms. The high ceilings and thick walls help maintain the coolness; rising hot air is vented through small openings located at the top of the exterior walls. The need for cooling the *dar* is given primary consideration over the need for heating. The *dars* are cold in the winter, even with doors and windows closed and heavy carpets rolled onto the floors.

The courtyard provides for outdoor privacy in a dense urban setting where the public domain infringes upon the individual and constantly threatens the sense of peace and tranquility. This open space also echoes the notion of centrality and control that is such a vital cultural symbol and belief in Morocco.

106

COURTYARD
GARDENS

Two different types of Moroccan garden, the *ouest ed-dar* (patio) and the *riyad*, occupy the central building courtyard. The simpler patio is generally paved, not planted, while the larger *riyad* can have elaborate beds of flowering and scented plants or citrus trees. Whatever their size or type, these Moroccan gardens use common elements to create oases of peace and comfort in a harsh environment.

In some courtyards, there may be a fountain (*seqqaya*) decorated with tiled *zellij* on one of the walls. In others, there will be a marble fountain (*khassa*) in the center. Water is the ultimate luxury in this arid environment, a symbol of life and abundance and of paradise on earth. This precious resource is used carefully; the flow is often modest, but it is contained in beautifully carved basins and fountains, allowed to brim over the edge into an overflow basin in a symbolic expression of plenty. Often, one of the basins is in the shape of an octagon, symbolic of the eightfold nature of the Islamic paradise.

Water is used to delight the senses. The sound of water reinforces the feeling of calm and the illusion of plenty in this hot, dry climate. It serves to mask the sounds of the crowded city beyond the walls of the *dar*. In some courtyards, the water ripples and flows in the basin and reflects glints of light, adding movement and sparkle to the static environment. Or the water may be dark and quiet, a meditation on the infinite nature of the Almighty.

The desert environment offers extremes of heat and cold. The light and heat of the sun are harvested and manipulated to contribute to the thermal comfort of the house. Light plays an important role, with designers taking advantage of it to define spaces and make use of it as a decorative element. Stone grilles and wood screens, called *moucharaby*, catch the sun, throwing intricate

shadows across the floors and walls. Shards of light reflect off the water in central basins, dancing along walls and ceilings. The highly polished stone and tile surfaces gleam in the sunlight.

Light is also important in defining interior spaces. The effect begins at the front door, which separates the bright public street from the darker residential interior. The arcades surrounding the courtyard form the second stage of transformation from public to private, their shadowy spaces encircling the brighter semiprivate arena of the patio. As one moves from the sunlit open area into the shadows, one enters the privacy of the interior rooms.

The extent of the adornment in the *dar* courtyard reflects the family's position, while in the medersa and the mosque, religious tradition dictates the use of color and ornament. Typically, the walls and floor of the courtyard are decorated with marble stones or *zellij*. The ingenuity of the craftsman is demonstrated by the color patterns and combinations. Brightly colored tile decorations can simulate the sensory experience of a garden without the water needed to maintain living flowers and shrubs. The colors in the human habitat of the courtyard contrast with the monochromatic landscape and provide a simple and effective means of creating the illusion of lushness and keeping the desert at bay.

Tile work is not the only choice for decoration in the courtyard. White and colored plaster panels, often carved into complex shapes, are also used to add interest to the interior space. *Moucharaby* screens add texture and shadow as they separate interior and exterior space. Colored glass panels (*chemmassiat*) inserted in the plaster walls soften the intense light coming from outside. Whatever the material used, it is generally worked to a smooth surface; rough textures are seldom seen in the courtyard because smooth surfaces reflect the sun and are cooler to the touch.

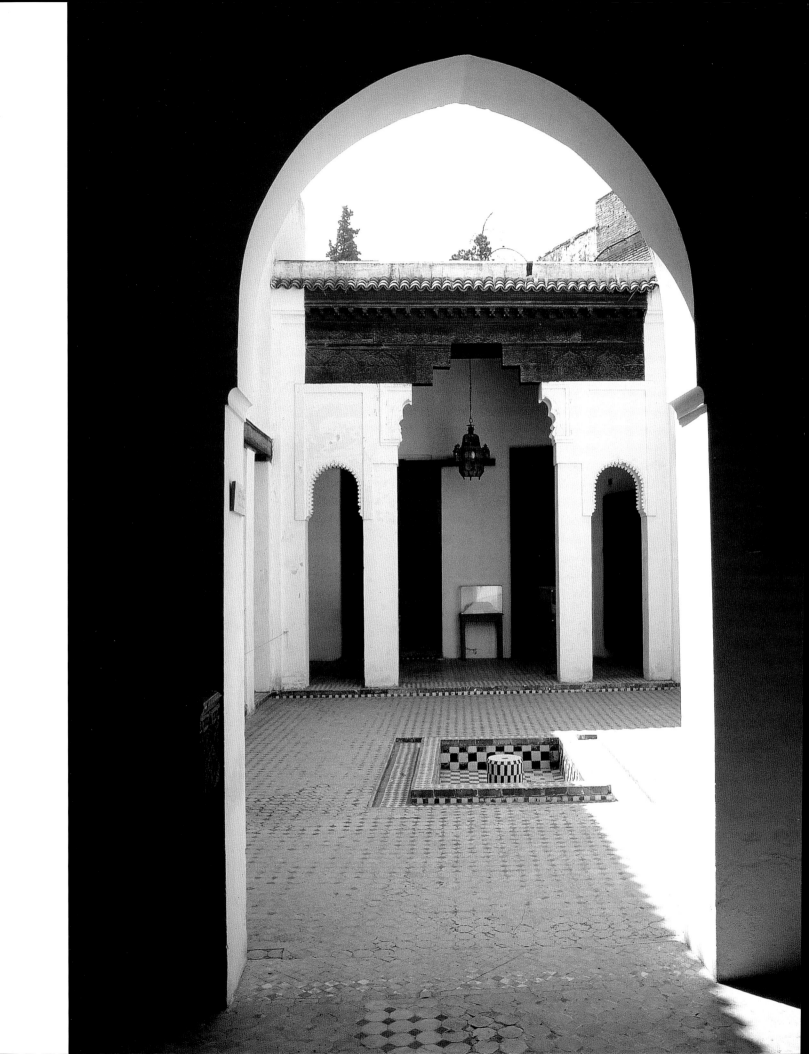

THE MOSQUE
COURTYARD

In Islam, the act of individual prayer and communication with God can take place anywhere, since the whole earth is viewed as God's abode. The mosque, however, is the place of communal worship, the site of Friday prayers, and the place where students and strangers come together. It is therefore also a public dwelling space.

The mosque is often organized around an interior courtyard (*sahn*) with an arched portico surrounding the customary ablution pool (*midha*). The prayer hall typically has a T shape, with the central aisle leading to the *mihrab*. The pulpit (*minbar*) is usually located to the right. The minaret located at an exterior corner of the mosque is typically square and constructed of stone with one or more openings, decorated facades, and a *jamour*, a spire of graduated copper spheres.

The courtyard (*sahn*) and the prayer hall are the principal spaces within the mosque. The courtyard can be square or rectangular, and it often has a basin in the middle for purification and ablutions. The prayer hall usually contains furnishings such as a pulpit, a Koran stand, and cabinets.

Mosques often have green-tiled roofs and the unobtrusive and restrained public facade typical of Moroccan structures. As an expression of its true functional meaning, the mosque fits into the urban pattern, neither detached from other buildings nor overly monumental. It is the mosque's interior ornamentation that consecrates the place. When the decorations are subdued, the space becomes emphasized, with the void becoming the manifestation of the force of the Almighty.

Courtyard of a medersa in Salé. Lower walls are covered with zellij tiles in a variety of geometric motifs, upper walls are plaster carved into an airy filigree, and wood panels accent the tops of the walls, lintels, and courtyard ceilings.

KAIROUINE MOSQUE

FEZ

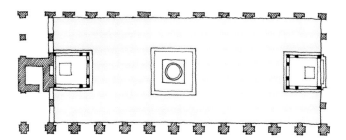

The Kairouine oratory was founded in 857 by Fatima, the daughter of Muhammad El-Fahri, a rich refugee from Kairouan, Tunisia, who had fled to Morocco from his native city with other residents. The Kariouine quarter of Fez is named for these early refugees.

The original building consists of a prayer hall with four aisles, each with twelve arched bays. In 956, the minaret was constructed by the Berber emirs who ruled Cordoba. It is a slender, twenty-three-meter high structure whose base is a square five meters on a side. The emir created the new *sahn* (interior courtyard) and enlarged the prayer hall, where the Friday sermon has been delivered ever since. In 1135 the Almoravid sultan Ali Ben Youssef extended and rebuilt the nave and installed an elaborate wooden *mihrab* created in a Cordoba workshop known for its superb craftsmanship. The sultan also added squinched domes with stalactite ornaments (*muqarnas*) carved in plaster. In 1289 the Merenid dynasty under the rule of Sultan Abu Yaqub Youssef added the library and covered the minaret with stucco to protect the limestone from deterioration. Three *medersas* (religious schools) were added to the complex in which the tradition of *halaqat* (study group) learning, a practice dating to the tenth century, was carried out. At the same period the galleries around the courtyard were redesigned and the mosque was embellished with ornate decorations and lamps. The last addition was made by the Saadian sultan Abdullah Ben Al Shaikh between 1613 and 1624. He constructed the two pavilions and the water features in the courtyard. Even now it is apparent that the building and its spaces were not conceived together, but rather accreted over time according to many different plans and aesthetic styles.

Today, the library of the mosque houses a collection of more than thirty thousand volumes of theological writings and ten thousand manuscripts, some extremely rare, including a fourteenth-century copy of the Koran made by Ibn Khaldun. The current prayer hall has eighteen aisles with twenty-one arched bays each and accommodates more than twenty thousand people. Approximately three hundred students are normally in residence at the *medersas* connected to the mosque.

Seventeen entrances to the mosque were built, of which fourteen are currently in use. The result of this porous design is to make the complex highly accessible from all parts of the city. The formal entry to the Kairouine Mosque runs through multiple doorways, making the transition through a sequence of spaces from the street to the main interior courtyard and then to the prayer hall. This progression slows the worshiper down, prepares him for the mood of a holy place, and removes him from the hectic hustle and bustle of life outside at the main gate to city and the street leading to the market. This movement into and through the space is analogous to opening and closing doors in a home: it allows the visitor to transition from space to space, function to function, and mood to mood.

The courtyard measures about 43 meters by 16 meters, a proportion of about three to one. Its size contrasts strongly with the extremely large enclosed interior space of the mosque, whose overall dimensions are 90 meters by 67 meters, of which more than two-thirds is occupied by the prayer hall. These dimensions are important. The courtyard space is neither so small as to become an air well, nor so large than it can no longer relate intimately to the structure. While the courtyard is open, the space is not infinite; it only implies the boundless through its suggestion of spaces beyond and its view of the dome of the sky above.

The courtyard is defined by the walls of the mosque—the exterior walls of the building as well as the interior walls of the courtyard itself. The colonnaded passage along the entryway is a place for quiet conversations and is always populated by visitors. The women's entrance to the mosque is from the far side of the colonnade since there is no mixing of the sexes within.

The long side of the courtyard boasts seven pilasters, while the short side has five. The entrance is off the short axis, with the result that the major axis is perpendicular to main line of movement. Two pavilions, their roofs perched on slender marble pillars, project into the courtyard from both sides and define the main axis; the separation helps to create a sense of spaciousness. Within each pavilion and at the center of the courtyard are fountains for ritual ablutions. The pavilion fountains are about two meters in diameter, each sitting in a basin approximately three meters square. The main fountain, made of marble, sits in the middle of the courtyard in a square of about seven meters, surrounded by a recessed drainage channel a few centimeters wide. An elevated square marble basin four meters across stands in the middle of the square. A cylindrical pedestal carries a scalloped marble basin filled to the brim with constantly flowing water. By physically raising these elements above the surface of the courtyard, the designer has emphasized their special qualities and their ritual function.

In the courtyards of most other religious buildings in Morocco, the pavement is simple, and the vertical surfaces provide the ornamental details and visual interest. In this mosque, however, the horizontal surfaces are also delineated and detailed. The floor tiles are set in a diamond pattern on the diagonal, with alternating large and small squares and eight-sided stars in between. The diagonal axis and size variation in the tiles creates a sense of movement. The busy pattern makes this a space that is not relaxed, despite the fact that it is peaceful and quiet most of the time. The tile pattern catches the light and dazzles the viewer. The white reflective surface of the wall and the use of white tiles in the pavement make the courtyard feel clean, in contrast to the street. Shoes are removed outside at the gate;

this action emphasizes the interior quality of the space and the carpet-like surface.

The white and the blue of the tiles give an airy feeling as if one is connected to the patch of sky bordered by the roof tiles above. The mosque's green roofs, visible from everywhere in the city, have a glossy emerald surface that is very attractive in the dusty hot environment. This color is reminiscent of the green of the orange-tree leaves, allowing the tiles to create an illusion of a vegetative canopy.

The columns inside the mosque and in the courtyard are set in recurring patterns and rhythms and give a strong order to the space. Inside the mosque, this formal design emphasizes man-made control, mirroring the order of the religious ritual, which is highly structured. Outside, the effect is different, creating a place where the faithful can reflect and worship privately. Inside, the mosque is controlled by religious rules. Outside is a retreat from forced organization. Worship here is contemplative, individual, and open to sky and emphasizing a personal relationship to the world and to nature.

The use of the space in the courtyard appears uneven and somewhat random, with most congregating taking place near the two pavilions. In this courtyard people inhabit the edges and corners more than the center. This is partially in response to the heat and the bright light and partly because the surface pattern encourages movement quickly across the short axis from the main gate to the fountain for ablutions before prayer, or to find refuge in one of the pavilions at either end. The elongated north-south orientation means that there is usually a shaded path or sitting area; only at noon is the courtyard fully in the sun.

This mosque, which is one of the largest and most revered religious centers in the Maghreb, is also one of those closest to the ideals of the culture. The understated structure on the outside hides the elaborate and ornate indoors, in order to preserve the harmony and modesty of the community. The hints at ornamentation in the courtyards, the limited space allotted for individual reflection, and the connection between the individual, the community, and the open air parallel the way *dars* and *riyads* are used in daily life.

KUTUBIYYA MOSQUE

MARRAKECH

The Almohad Berber caliph Abd el Moumen built the original Kutubiyya Mosque in 1147 after establishing his capital at Marrakech. This first mosque was destroyed a few years later when it was discovered that it had been positioned incorrectly in relation to Mecca. Rebuilding of the mosque began in 1160, based on the original design but with the orientation corrected. The project was finally completed in 1199 by el Moumen's grandson, Yacoub el Mansour.

Kutubiyya means "the Mosque of the Booksellers" and refers to the *kutubiyin*, sellers of manuscripts who displayed their wares on stalls in the square in front of the mosque's entrance. By locating the mosque in the booksellers' market and naming it after them, the caliph was emphasizing the importance of literacy to his dynasty and the life of the country.

The mosque was at one time one of the largest in the Islamic world with total area of 5,400 square meters. The plan follows the traditional design of a rectangular colonnaded hall. It has sixteen parallel aisles of identical size and one wider central aisle perpendicular to the *qibla* wall that faces Mecca. A 77-meter-high minaret of rose-colored sandstone towers above the mosque and the city to become the most important landmark, a welcoming sign for visitors who approach Marrakech. The minaret is topped by a decorated lantern and a ribbed cupola. The tower is 12.5 meters wide and 67.5 meters high to the top of the cupola, closely approximating the one-to-five ratio considered to produce the most harmonious proportion. Ornamental stone panels carved with lacy, intricate designs cover the minaret, each side displaying a different pattern.

The Kutubiyya minaret is one of only three minarets in this classic Moroccan-Andalusia style of architecture that still exist today. The second is part of the Hassan mosque in Rabat, which was built to a height of 44 meters but never completed. The third and most impressive is at La Giralda in Seville, the surviving part of the great mosque built by the Almohad sultan Abu Ya'qub Yusuf in the twelfth century. Originally 82 meters high, La Giralda's minaret is now more than 100 meters tall as the result of additions made when it was incorporated into the nearby cathedral.

At the foot of the Kutubiyya mosque stands the tomb of Lalla Zohra, a white *koubba* built in the seventeenth century for the daughter of a slave who became a religious leader. The tomb has become an important place of pilgrimage for Marrakech's female worshipers.

The mosque and the tall decorated minaret dominate the outdoor space adjacent to the prayer hall, an enclosed courtyard of approximately 50 by 20 meters. A fountain set on a small square base is located in the center at the entrance to the middle aisle. Only remnants of *zellij* decoration that once ornamented the courtyard remain as a result of heavy use. Unlike most mosque courtyards, the Kutubiyya's outdoor space is planted, with twenty-four orange trees set in a grid of small rectangular tree wells spaced across the courtyard. This courtyard is similar to the medieval Patios de los Naranjos in Seville and Córdoba. The Spanish courtyards are bigger and more formal than the one at the Kutubiyya, with their numerous trees and the accentuated irrigation channels representing a formal conceptual translation of an orchard into a three-dimensional design, the trees fulfilling symbolic and decorative functions. The Kutubiyya courtyard, on the other hand, was designed modestly as an intimate *riyad*— more an actual orchard than an abstraction, a place where the

Men resting in the shade at midday.

LEFT
View of the mosque and courtyard from the minaret.

trees bear fruit to be eaten and provide shade for the comfort of visitors. Even now, when the pavement is no longer covered with climate-moderating tiles, the courtyard's function in protecting worshipers from the heat of the day and the cold of the night is the determining force behind its design. The intimate size and neglected nature of the space have allowed it to become a refuge, a safe haven where male visitors can congregate in groups of two or three. During the day, some lie on the cool, hard pavement under the dark shadows of the trees, while others sit around the simple pool to meditate and converse. At night the pavement remains warm from the heat of the sun, and it continues to be used as a place to rest and socialize.

Both the inside and the outside of the Kutubiyya display the result of man's interaction with the natural elements. The builders used natural forms to embellish the stones in order to create a man-made, urban landscape. Within the courtyard, the designer emphasized the growing of plants and used their color to adorn the monotonous and hard surroundings. Enclosed on all sides with no decoration save the dark shiny leaves of the orange trees, the Kutubiyya courtyard is the closest urban approximation to a Moroccan orchard. The entire complex is a wonderful example of the Moroccan-Andalusian way of combining austerity and simplicity with superb craftsmanship. The enchanting atmosphere is communicated viscerally rather than intellectually, and therefore is able to clearly convey the culture of the people.

THE MEDERSA COURTYARD

The *medersa* is a semipublic residence for theology students, often situated beside a mosque. Most *medersas* in good condition have been in continuous use since the thirteenth and fourteenth centuries, and thus reflect primarily the ornate style of the Merenid rulers of that time. The buildings of the *medersa* usually surround an open courtyard containing a central pool of water for the performance of ritual ablutions. The *medersa* is the public *dar*, the home away from home for the scholars.

The interior courtyard is generally flanked on three sides by student cells. A prayer or teaching hall is located on the fourth side opposite the ornate entrance door. The cells on the second level open to a narrow gallery, which is sometimes completely covered. The residential students and the believers, supported by wealthy patrons, live in cells measuring approximately one and a half by two meters. The pavement and the decoration can range from simple patterns constructed in marble to intricate ornate *zellij*. Carved plaster and wood are often added on the vertical surfaces for decoration.

The Bou Inania Medersa is a noted example of Merenid architecture.

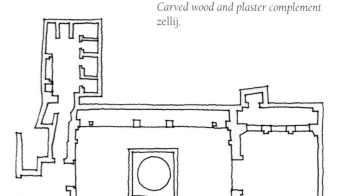

ATTARINE MEDERSA

FEZ

The Attarine Medersa was constructed between 1323 and 1325 by the Merenid sultan Abu Said and was named after the Perfume and Spices ("Attarine") Souk where it is located. The *medersa* was built in close proximity to the Kairouine Mosque and was originally intended to be the college of the mosque, designated as a dormitory for about sixty students who came mostly from northwest Morocco. The Attarine Medersa was in use as a school until the early twentieth century.

The design of the structure follows the traditional pattern. It includes the vestibule, which creates a transitional space between the quiet *medersa* and the bustling street outside. A corridor leads from the front entrance through the living space and then to a staircase to the upper story. A prayer hall sits directly across the courtyard from the entrance, and student cells are located around the periphery of the courtyard on both the first and second floors. The lodgings are screened from the visitors by elaborate wooden *moucharaby* panels. Like other *medersas*, the Attarine follows the practice of creating an ornate public space in the courtyard and placing stark and spartan student accommodations within the shell of the building.

The Attarine Medersa is a small, irregularly shaped structure roughly 16 by 32 meters in extent, with a courtyard of 12 by 16 meters. However, the small scale is offset by exuberant and intricate decorations. Narrow, 2-meter-wide aisles on each long side of the courtyard are supported by rectangular pillars faced with tile and carved stucco. In the center and at each long end are two slender marble and alabaster columns that carry symmetrical wooden arches above. The blind wooden facade of the upper story repeats in scale and size the carved stucco arches below. The cedar wood, *zellij*, and carved plaster that cover the walls, the rectangular columns, and the pavement are all rendered in geometric shapes in combinations of five-, eight-, ten-, and sixteen-pointed stars. The concept of squaring the circle is seen everywhere. Square forms appear on the horizontal planes, while round shapes predominate on the vertical surfaces. Floral shapes are mostly found on the walls and above the entrance to the prayer hall. The floral motifs are anchored by the solid geometry below in a pattern that echoes the order of nature—solid in the earth, floral and loose at the top, reaching to the sky.

The play between the square and the circle is employed in the design of the water source. A circular marble fountain with an edge of eight scallops is located in the middle of the courtyard, providing the water for ablution and cooling. A white marble square, a barely noticeable depression in the floor, holds the basin and sets the water source apart from the rest of the pavement, which is tiled in diagonally set blue squares. The basin's depressed circular base is paved in black, sandalwood, white, and green tiles in three concentric circles. The tiles closest to the water are small squares set on the diagonal, and the farthest circle is covered in geometric tiles that create an abstract floral pattern.

The central volume of the open courtyard engulfs visitors as they enter and pass through to the prayer hall. The filigree work on the walls, so delicately and elaborately produced, and the colorful *zellij* give a sense of luxurious domesticity more in keeping with a prosperous residence than with a religious school and community prayer hall.

Square tiles on lower panels symbolize the earth, while white plaster lifts the gaze toward the sky; slender alabaster columns contrast with the robust patterns of the tiles.

126

Cedar canopy over the courtyard admits light and casts shadows across the decoration.

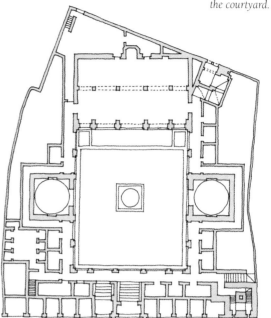

BOU INANIA MEDERSA

FEZ

Similar to the Attarine Medersa in style and opulence is the Bou Inania Medersa, located in the western part of Fez el-Bali. It was constructed by Abu Inan between 1350 and 1357 A.D. As was often the case, the sultan was the patron of the *medersa* and was responsible for the construction of the buildings, provision of running water, maintenance of the structures, and the administration of the institution, including providing faculty salaries and student stipends.

Because of its distance from the Kairouine Mosque and the absence of other mosques nearby at the time of construction, the *medersa* became an institution unto itself, containing extremely small and austere student cells (intended for sleeping and studying only); a mosque, minaret, and *minbar* for the Friday sermon; and a public cemetery. In addition, to one side of the back entrance was a religious school for children, while the front facade contained shops and a public latrine. The various activities accommodated by this institution essentially made Bou Inania a community center, a broad concept of a house of worship that is rooted in the traditions of Islam.

The *medersa* complex also contained a large and very unusual medieval water clock (located on the building opposite the main entrance) that was built by the sultan Abu Said in 1317 and restored by the sultan Abu Inan as construction on the *medersa* was completed. The clock punctuated the time for prayer in the *medersa* as well as signaling the time for praying for other mosques in the city by hoisting a flag. Although the clock has fallen into disrepair, efforts are underway to restore it to its original state as part of the project to save the cultural monuments in the Fez *medina*.

The sober exterior facade of the *medersa* blends with the rest of the city; the entrance is noticeable only because of its projecting portal. Below a panel ornamented with filigree is a skillfully carved cedar gate that does not reach the arch of the building. This ingenious design creates a dark background to the gate as one looks from the courtyard toward the entrance and lets light come from the courtyard to the public vestibule when the gate is closed, thus suggesting the high level of craftsmanship within.

Two staircases in the main entrance lead to the second floor of the building. One is intended for use only by those who have washed their bare feet with the water from a nearby wall fountain or in the central fountain in the courtyard. Along the stairs immediately upon entering are benches for visitors to sit and watch the play of shadows over the courtyard and the reflections in the mirrorlike fountain in the middle. This vestibule extends the experience of passing from the noisy bazaar to the peaceful interior space.

After entering the courtyard, visitors must cross the open space axially to the prayer hall, another spatial device to calm and slow the people while preparing them to communicate with their creator. There are two points of water in the courtyard; one is a slightly depressed circular fountain while the other is a water channel that runs across the facade of the prayer hall, terminating in a marble slab at each end. While the main function of the channel is providing water for ablutions and evaporative cooling, it also separates the prayer hall from the courtyard and purposefully delineates the transition from the profane to the sacred space.

Each *medersa* or mosque uses a specific design element to stress the singularity and the importance of the institution. In

*The simple street facade belies
the elaborate structure within.*

RIGHT
*Carved cedar panels shield the
passage around the courtyard
from the elements.*

Bou Inania, the contrast between the vertical and the horizontal plane of the courtyard is accentuated. The courtyard facade is a harmonious combination of materials, textures, and colors with no dominating force, all in abundance, all in order. In contrast to this ornate facade, whose woodcarving, plasterwork, tiles, and architectural details are perfectly formed, the pavement is made of simple light-colored marble tiles, slightly unmatched in size, giving the impression that the stones were found and laid casually in place rather than skillfully cut. This contrasting design and materials reflect the view that both the natural and the cultural elements need to be given form in a place that glorifies Allah. The complex in its entirety becomes a testament to the deity who instills the ability in his believers to do such intricate work.

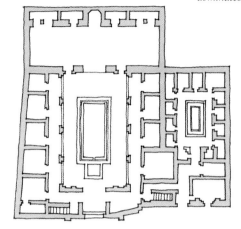

The medersa *is named for the* pool, *or* sahar, *that dominates its courtyard.*

SAHRIJ MEDERSA

FEZ

The Sahrij Medersa was constructed by Sultan Abul Hassan and was inaugurated in 1323. Located in Fez el-Bali near the Andalusian Mosque, it served as the hostel for the students who were connected to this mosque. The name Sahrij (from the root *sahar*, to melt something, used in architecture to mean a water tank) refers to the white marble basin in the courtyard.

The entry courtyard is an enclosed, semi-public space. Its small size and elaborated entrance reinforce the sense of privacy. From the street, visitors pass first through the covered passage and then take a small step down to the patio, the subtle variation in level preparing the visitors to enter the space. The courtyard itself is about 10 by 20 meters in size. The central rectangular pool, about 5 by 10 meters, reflects the ornate wood and stucco facade worked in the Merenid style. The pool acts as a mirror that enlarges the space and adds depth and dimension. The reflections in the water change constantly, depending on the vantage point and the varying light as the sun moves across the sky.

The water in the pool flows from a circular marble basin through a short, narrow channel. This fluted basin is located in a depressed circle, which in turn is surrounded by another depressed rectangular area. These minute details, with level changes on the order of a few centimeters, are magnified by the play of the sun. The shadows mark the objects and create a border around them, accentuating the details and adding interest to the horizontal surface.

Another semiprivate courtyard is located inside the *medersa* proper. It is smaller, about 400 square meters, and more intimate. It can be approached only through a side entrance and is surrounded by the students' living cells. A small pool about 2.5 by

5 meters, its shape echoing the larger basin in the first courtyard, is located in the middle of this space and was used by the students for performing ritual ablutions. In both courtyards, there is just enough space around the pools to allow visitors to move—between rooms in the small courtyard, or in and out of the arcade surrounding the entry courtyard of the prayer hall.

The upper surface of the interior facade of the courtyard is made of carved cedar planking. The *moucharaby* that cover the high windows add depth by creating a play of shadows that articulates the space. The lower facade is faced with a combination of plaster and wood worked in all the styles available to the craftsmen. The design is very intricate and combines floral, epigraphic, and geometrical figures. The lower part of the wall contains a geometric design, while the top features floral patterns with both smooth and striated leaves. Pinecone and palmetto motifs are repeated throughout the *medersa* and are seen prominently in the upper part of the building and at the entry to the prayer hall.

The *zellij* are the earliest of any in the Moroccan *medersas*, simple interlaced patterns based on an eight-point star. The *zellij* is rendered in hues of black, white, red, green, and blue, with a narrow green band and blue pinecone pattern on a white background along the vertical walls. The horizontal plane is made of squares of white and black tiles set on the diagonal with a band of green tile.

The restoration of the *medersa* and the entry courtyard has been done with care and skill. Its vividly colored tiles and ornate facade, domestic scale, and intricate wall decorations, evoke the living room of a large house, with a fine the carpet and artwork along the walls, rather than a public *medersa*.

136

BEN YOUSSEF MEDERSA

MARRAKECH

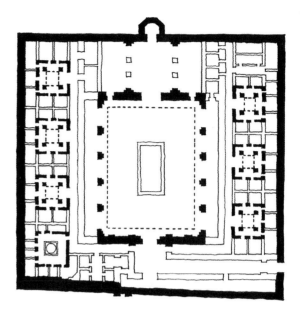

The Merenid sultan Abu El Hassan founded the Ben Youssef Medersa in the fourteenth century, naming it after the devout Sidi Youssef Ben Ali, one of the seven patron saints of the city. The dates 1564 and 1565 are incised on the old foundations. At that time, Marrakech was going through a building boom that attracted craftsmen from Córdoba, the rest of Europe, and the Middle East. The design and the use of materials in this and other institutions of the period represent the last surge of grand architecture in Marrakech. Restored in the 1960s with care and great skill, the *medersa* offers visitors a view of the late dynasty's opulent style and accomplished craftsmanship.

The entire *medersa* complex comprises a square of approximately 28 meters on each side. The main courtyard in the center of the building is about 15 meters square. Despite its square shape, the main courtyard gives the impression of a rectangular outdoor room. This illusion is created in part by two narrow colonnades that border the northeast and the southwest sides of the courtyard. These aisles provide a cool shaded place with a carpet-like *zellij* floor that invites visitors to sit and rest. The feeling of an elongated space is also enhanced by the position of the prayer hall along the axis, which draws visitors' attention directly into the hall, especially when the main door is ajar.

The visual rectangularity of the space is reinforced by the reflecting pool located in the middle of the courtyard. A narrow channel around the pool creates a shadow that accentuates its shape. Unlike a central fountain or a reflecting pool pushed to one side of the space, the large rectangular reflecting pool in the center of the courtyard interrupts the passage through the space and encourages lingering and exploration. As visitors sit down, their eyes become riveted to the ever-changing reflections of the

building in the water and the patterns of light and shadows that dance on the courtyard floor.

The entrance leads from the street through a narrow dark corridor to a square vestibule with a monumental carved cedar door in the style of the Fez *medersas*. At this point the visitor can choose to enter the courtyard and the prayer hall, walk down a corridor to the students' cells, or climb separate stairs to the cells on the upper story.

The *medersa* housed as many as nine hundred students at one time in its warrens of tiny cells. The cells cluster around seven inner courtyards. Some of the second-story cells open directly onto the upper gallery, while others have access to view and ventilation only through very small openings on the outer walls of the *medersa*. One of the seven student courtyards contains the latrines and the ablution pool.

The pyramid roofs of the prayer hall and the main entrance are made of glossy green tiles. The same tiles cover the angled roofs around the courtyard openings, which are designed to shed the rainwater in two directions, down into the smaller courtyards on each side. The curved roof tiles create an undulating fringe to the openings, and the sinuous shadows are marked on the courtyard's floor by the changing position of the sun.

All available surfaces of the *medersa,* except for the marble pavement in the main courtyard, are covered with decorations. The lower part of the vertical walls of the aisles, the lower part of the columns, and the inside walls of the pool are sheathed with intricate multicolored *zellij* in eight-point-star patterns. Above the *zellij* are bands of sandalwood-colored tiles with black floral cursive inscriptions. A white pinecone shape on black background tiles separates this row in turn from the next band.

LEFT
The medersa *is known for its elaborate columns decorated in* zellij *and incised calligraphy.*

FACING PAGE
Calligraphic inscriptions dedicated to Ali Ben Youssef, one of the seven patron saints of the city.

Upper gallery leading to student cells.

FOLLOWING PAGES
Pages 144-145: Particularly rich decoration in the courtyard.

Pages 146-147: Light plays on delicate tracery.

Elaborate floral script carved in red plaster terminates the lower decorations. The upper part of the walls and columns are decorated in filigreed stucco and culminate in carved cedar lintels and horizontal panels. The dark heavy timber visually lowers the wall and brings the sky closer to the floor of the courtyard.

The entire school is oriented inward toward the courtyards and appears to be a self-contained unit, cut off from the surrounding neighborhood. By enclosing and shielding the residents on all sides and the creating the illusion of low ceilings, the courtyard provides a sheltering space that exudes a feeling of repose and stability.

Among the decorative writing on the walls there is an inscription dedicated to the sultan who founded the *medersa*. It reads: "I was constructed as a place of knowledge and prayer by the Prince of the Faithful, the descendant of the seal of the prophets, Abdallah, the most glorious of Caliphs. Pray for him, all ye who enter here, so that his greatest hopes may be realized."

THE FUNDUQ

In times past, caravanserais were places of rest and shelter constructed at intervals of one day's walk along the trade routes of the Middle East and Africa. These buildings usually comprised one to three stories of small individual rooms surrounding a typical open courtyard.

The word "caravanserai" is derived from the Persian "*karawan*," a company of travelers, and "*serai*," large inn. In most places, the inns were built and maintained by the rulers of the area, who also provided wells and cisterns to aid the traveling merchants and pilgrims and to encourage trade. In Morocco these institutions were usually sponsored by a religious organization and became known as *funduqs*. The *funduqs* were usually built near a city's main gate in order to be convenient for travelers. In the past, the first-floor rooms of a *funduq* were reserved for storage of the traders' merchandise. The courtyard was the public meeting place and also the place to house the travelers' animals. Upper levels were reserved for the travelers' lodging.

Certain *funduqs* were established to house Christian and Jewish traders. Since local laws forbade non-Muslims to set up their stalls in the souk, they instead conducted trade within their *funduqs*. Over time, other groups began to use the *funduqs* for selling and trading. Although some *funduqs* still serve as inns today, in most cities they have evolved into permanent trade centers devoted to a particular kind of merchandise.

In most cities in Morocco today, one can find a *funduq* of seeds, leather, ceramics, carpets, and even of books. The merchandise is generally stored on the first floor at the street level, with the upper stories rented as lodgings or used for longer-term storage. Animals are no longer kept in the courtyards, which are now reserved for business, since they are located in the desirable area near the principal city gate and usually in close proximity to the main souk. The courtyard in both commercial *funduqs* and inns is usually constructed of rammed earth and not paved with tile as in other courtyard buildings. A well, cistern, or fountain will be located in the courtyard or near the entrance, and a set of large balancing scales is often fixed to the wall to help measure the purchased goods. An awning or a grapevine covering a wood or bamboo trellis provides some shade as the merchants conduct their business. Other *funduq* inns have been converted into hotels and restaurants, with their courtyards becoming integral parts of their operation.

The city of Fez was once home to hundreds of commercial and residential *funduqs*. About 270 of these structures have been slated for renovation as part of the citywide restorations. Today, the Najjarin (carpenters') Funduq is the best known in Fez. Built in 1711 by Amin Adiyil, it is located between the carpenters' and the henna souks in close proximity to the Attarine (perfumers') and Kissarine (shoemakers') souks. Massive double doors, wide enough to allow heavily laden animals to enter, mark its entrance, with smaller doorways set in the larger panels for those who travel by foot. The four-story structure has three or four rooms on a side, each opening onto an internal gallery that overlooks the central courtyard. The rooms are very plain on the inside, but on the outside are heavy cedar beams,

View of the upper galleries. Najjarin Funduq.

RIGHT
Funduq *still in use as a warehouse for wool.*

geometric latticework railings, and skillfully executed carved wood screens.

The interior courtyard once had a fountain in the center and a wall fountain situated outside the portal. Today only the tiled wall fountain remains, its intricate geometric pattern and colors the focal point of the square and a landmark for the entire city. The Najjarin Funduq is the most complete structure of its kind in Morocco today. It has been carefully restored and is now a museum where visitors can explore and appreciate the splendor and skill of the original design.

PALACE GARDENS

The palace (*kasr*) or grand house is generally a complex of buildings and pavilions formed from the integration of many *dars*, with several courtyards for public and private use, segregated by gender. The planted courtyards, (*riyads*) and the luxuriant gardens (grand *riyads*) of rulers and wealthy citizens are laid out according to traditional principles. Intersecting pathways divide the space into four plots, or multiples of four. The path is usually raised 25 to 50 centimeters above the ground, allowing flood irrigation in the planted areas and providing shade for the roots of the plants. Trees, shrubs, and carefully arranged perennials are packed into the small planting areas, creating an illusion of abundance, especially when seen from the walkway or from the house. Fountains are located at the center of the quadrants or at the intersection of the paths. Whichever design tradition is followed, plants in Moroccan courtyard gardens are usually either edible or fragrant and tend to come from a limited palette of species.

Orange and lemon trees (*Citrus sinensis* and *C. limon*; *naranshi* and *laymūn* in Arabic) are found in almost every *riyad*. Basil (*Ocimum basilicum*; *rihan*), oregano (*Origanum vulgare*; *anrar*), lilies (*Lilium spp.*; *susan*), lemon balm (*Melissa officinalis*), saffron crocus (*Crocus sativus*; *za'farân*), and other fragrant herbs and medicinal plants are planted in the earth or in pots scattered around the courtyard.

Most of the commonly used species are not native, but they have been in cultivation long enough to have developed cultural significance and meaning. Some of the plants came with the Phoenicians and the Romans, others were brought by the Arabs and the returning Moors, while still others arrived with the colonial powers in the twentieth century. Plants from California, Chile, and other arid zones in the Americas, as well as Australia, have been used heavily throughout the country, both for ornamentation and as sources for fruits and seasonings.

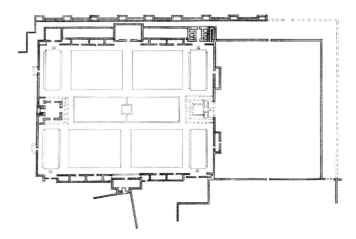

EL BADI PALACE

MARRAKECH

In 1578, the Portuguese king Sebastian I and his army landed on the Moroccan shore, intent on extending their control over the African country. In Ksar el Kebir, they clashed with Moroccan forces in the famous "Battle of the Three Kings." The Portuguese army was defeated in this bloody battle in which the three warring kings—Sebastian, Abd el Malik, and Moulay Mohammed—died on the battlefield. As a result of their defeat, the Portuguese were forced to cede control of their trading centers on the Atlantic coast and pay reparations to the Moroccans.

The Saadian sultan Ahmed al-Mansour ed-Dahbi ("the Golden") ascended to the throne after the battle and built the El Badi palace to commemorate the victory over the Portuguese. The construction of the palace was financed partly by the Portuguese reparations. The complex took nearly twenty-five years to complete, from 1578 to 1602, and survived intact from 1594 until 1708, when it was looted by Moulay Ismail to provide materials for his palace in the new capital city of Meknès.

The name El Badi means "the incomparable," making a connection between the ninety-nine names of Allah and the grandeur of the palace. Another meaning of the name relates to the palace's once elaborate decoration. *Ilm el badi** is the art of stylistic ornament, and the palace was certainly one of the most decorated in its day. Flowing Arabic calligraphy above one of the main gates expresses the designers' intent: "This gate is as beautiful as the eloquent beginning of a fine poem, and the palace is as the continuation of this poem." Although the palace's name suited the elegance and importance of the new complex, in Islamic numerology the name El Badi was discovered to be highly inauspicious. The value of its letters is 117, which would prove to be

exactly the number of lunar years (from 1002 AH to 1119 AH) the palace would remain intact.

The immense palace was alleged to have more than 360 rooms and audience halls. Ahmed al-Mansour was influenced by Ottoman court traditions and strove to make this palace the physical embodiment of his dynasty. Mansour recruited master craftsmen from Europe as well as from Africa and the Middle East and instructed them to use the most expensive materials to create decorated glazed tile, marble columns, carved stucco, and carved wooden ceilings. They imported wood, gold, ivory, onyx, and pure black and white marble from as far as Timbuktu, India, and Carrara, Italy. Sugar produced in the Sous region, a rare and desirable commodity, was exchanged pound for pound for the Italian marble.

In 1708, Moulay Ismail began raiding the palace and stripping it of its decorations and precious materials. For more than ten years, Moulay Ismail's builders scavenged the rich site, leaving only the skeleton of the formerly magnificent palace in its place.

Even though only scattered ruins of the palace, stables, and dungeons remain, with only few broken fragments of *zellij* to hint at the original elaborate decoration, the complex is still impressive in its scale and the simplicity of the design. Massive walls of rammed earth and remnants of the palace walls enclose an open court of approximately 140 by 110 meters. The courtyard is divided into sections by water channels that connect its five pools, with the large central pool measuring approximately 22 by 90 meters. The smaller basins, about 18 by 32 meters each, are located close to the eastern and western walls. The largest basin contains an island in the center. Four sunken parterres planted

with orange trees are framed by raised walkways that allow one to stroll among the pools and the planted areas; in true classical Persian style, the design creates the impression of walking on a living carpet.

A large pavilion is situated in the middle of each of the garden's four walls. The pavilions on the northern and the southern walls are recessed into the stone, while those on the western and eastern walls project into the courtyard. The large pavilion (nearly 12 meters on a side) positioned in the middle of the two pools on the west is called the Kubbat Khamsiniya after its fifty marble columns. It was used as a great reception hall on state occasions. In the middle of the pavilion are the remnants of a large fountain.

The design of the El Badi courtyard follows the rules of most private *riyads*, with the scale magnified tenfold. This expanded scale creates a massive void, which inspires a sense of awe and respect more profound than that evoked by many prayer halls and monumental mosques. The space is especially impressive when experienced in the context of the city, with its narrow streets, cramped living quarters, and thick walls. The feeling of complete removal from everyday life is intensified in the sunken orange groves, where the garden becomes a shady, fragrant retreat. Each section of the garden can be experienced individually, and yet each unit reinforces the totality of the space.

The various elements of the courtyard contribute to a sense of peace and tranquility. The massive red walls divide the inner space from the bustling world outside, establishing a sense of separation and a feeling of stability. The shiny green carpet formed

156

*The island in the middle of the pool is
a retreat for meditation.*

LEFT
*The calm reflecting pool also
functions as a reservoir.*

by the crowns of the orange trees and the water in the large pools, rippling with the soft wind, remind one of the essential life-giving properties of plants and water in this arid zone. Magnificent storks have made their nests at the tops of the ruins; in their flight and their silhouettes against the ever-changing color of the sky, they add a touch of magic to the atmosphere of this site.

The restrained ambience of the courtyard encourages visitors to become quiet, to slow their gait or sit along the edges of the pools and sunken gardens and contemplate the transitory nature of human influence. Once the symbol of power and human ambition, the palace today is a testimony to the futility of war. The site evokes memories of imperial opulence while at the same time emphasizing the ultimate lack of meaning in all such decoration.

EL BAHIA PALACE

MARRAKECH

In 1866, Si Moussa, the grand vizier to Sidi Mohammed ben Abd er-Rahman, built a palace for his family in the city of Marrakech. His son Ba Ahmed, vizier to the sultans Moulay Abd al-Azia and Abu er-Rahman, made plans to expand the original site, buying sixty buildings and sixteen garden plots in the vicinity and assembling a parcel that would allow him to create an extensive palace complex. Beginning in 1894, a thousand of the best craftsmen in Morocco worked on the palace for seven years according to a plan designed by the vizier's architect, El Haj Mohammed El Mekki. Working in carved wood, plaster, stucco, Meknès marble, and Tetouan and Fez multicolored *zellij*, the craftsmen and builders created what was then perceived to be an Andalusia-inspired design.

The finished Bahia Palace was so luxurious that when the French established their control over Morocco in the early twentieth century they chose it as the home of their first resident general, Hubert Lyautey. Even today, foreign dignitaries are housed there on special occasions, and concerts are sometimes held in the main hall. The palace is built on one level as an assemblage of separate dwellings opening to inner courtyards of various sizes. Only one apartment—containing the master of the house's living and sleeping quarters—is located on the second floor, near the entrance to the compound. Although the major expansion was planned and executed as a single piece, the palace feels as if it had accreted, with rooms added here and there as new members joined the large household.

The organization of the entrances and doorways within the palace was designed to accommodate the three important principals of family life: the segregation of the sexes, the concern of the culture for strict separation of public and private, and the par-

tition of the dwellings of the various wives and concubines from each other. The four wives had separate quarters, with each of these dwelling places opening onto its own private courtyard. The quarters for the harem of twenty-four concubines were centered on a separate courtyard.

These represent only a few of the palace's courtyards, some large enough for public assemblies, such as the great marble courtyard; some small and intimate spaces, such as the small *riyad* located within the dwelling of the favorite; and some for family retreats, such as the grand *riyad*.

The grand *riyad* is built in the manner of a cloister. The space measures 30 by 40 meters and is divided by walkways into four equal rectangular plots with a fountain located at the intersection of the walkways. Two other small fountains are located at each end of the *riyad* in front of decorated *kubbas*, or garden pavilions. The sense of total enclosure and intimate space is enhanced by the ornate entrances and ornamented columns of the galleries

TOP
View through the building to the garden beyond.

ABOVE
A secluded corner, dappled with sunlight.

RIGHT
The vast courtyard serves as a reception area for the palace.

162

surrounding the *riyad*. Green and white *zellij*, low green-painted balustrades, and overgrown plants with glossy, striated green leaves create a lush and soothing atmosphere. The *riyad* exhibits the traditional Moroccan planting palette of cypress, citrus trees, palms, jasmine, and a few banana trees. However, over the years heat-tolerant plants from the Americas and South Africa have been added to the traditional plants; these imports—clivia, kafir lily, various hibiscus, liriope, aspidistra, philodendron, cordyline, aucuba, and other shade-loving shrubs and groundcovers—are prized for their glossy green leaves and for their abundant, fragrant flowers.

The opposite feeling is generated by the great marble courtyard, a large (30-by-50-meter) unplanted space surrounded by one-story structures. The expanse of smooth marble pavement captures the sun's heat and reflects it back in all directions. During the day, guests retreat to the shaded galleries, whose slender carved wood columns support the overhanging roof. On cold nights, the heat of the sun stored in the marble is released to the air, and the courtyard becomes a comfortable place to stroll, the marble providing a warm surface to sit on or walk barefoot. Three fountains, two slightly sunken and one elevated with an overflowing basin, provide comforting background sound. The roofs of the galleries are covered in green tiles, which can be seen from everywhere in the courtyard and act as an abstract substitute for plants. This courtyard, unlike the intimate grand *riyad*, is public and inclusive, an outdoor reception room for the palace, as well as outdoor space for the private quarters whose windows and doors open directly onto it. Square marble pavement pavers are bordered by small *zellij*, a special design that echoes the grand carpet on the main axis leading from the public entrance to the large hall opposite across the courtyard.

The inward-looking orientation of the palace and its myriad courtyards, the close relationship between indoor and outdoor rooms, and the microclimates provided by the arrangement of the structures combine to create a foil to the reality of life outside. In a crowded, chaotic, and noisy desert city, where one must constantly seek refuge, the Bahia Palace represents a model for constructing a unique haven for a large group of people living in close proximity to one another.

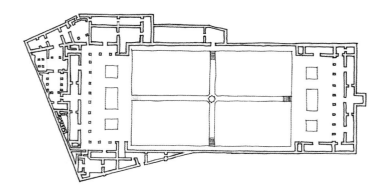

DAR BATHA

FEZ

Dar Batha is located at the eastern end of Fez el-Bali, south of Bab Bou Jeloud. Built by the sultan Moulay Hassan, who ruled from 1873 until 1894, the building was later enlarged by his successor, Moulay Abd al-Aziz.

The sultan originally built the complex as a palace for public audiences and assemblies. Today it houses a museum of traditional arts and crafts, including collections of Moroccan wrought iron artifacts, sculpted wood, embroidery, carpets, jewelry, and coins. In addition there are impressive collections of astronomical instruments and ceramic objects displaying the celebrated "Fez blue" ceramic work.

The palace was built as an enclosed compound. Only the roofs provide vantage points from which to view the surrounding city. The main residential section is located on the west side of the complex; on the east side, a separate building forms the fourth wall of the enclosure. Several courtyards in the main building serve as sources of ventilation and as the typical outdoor rooms found in even the most modest Moroccan homes.

The garden occupies the entire space between the two buildings, with a planted area of approximately 60 by 100 meters. Narrow decorated galleries run the length of the north and south walls. The extensive multicolored *zellij* work and the ornate roofs of the galleries create a man-made garden-like atmosphere that provides a transition from the buildings to the open space. Stairs lead down from the buildings to the sunken planted areas, and walkways traverse the space between the two galleries and the two structures, dividing the garden area into four sections. Since the walkways are all the same width, there is no hierarchy between the path joining the main structures and the path to the galleries. All are paved with brick set in a herringbone pattern edged with *zellij*.

The planted space below the walks is filled with a mixture of vegetation, both exotic and native. Oaks, cypresses, date palms, banana trees, and bamboo constitute the upper canopy. Rhododendron, cycads, lantana, salvia, and other perennials provide the ground cover. This abundance and variety of plants creates a dark and shady hideaway in the center of the complex.

At the edge of the garden are two identical terraces, one in front of each of the buildings; a third terrace of similar design stands on the roof of the eastern building. These terraces are paved in stone edged with a band of *zellij*. Tiled *zellij* bands mark the edges of each of the raised walls, the walkways, the steps, the pool, and both the gallery floors.

Two fountains and a small rectangular pool are situated in the centers of each of the three open paved areas. The fountains are set in ornate sunken basins, lavishly decorated in intricate *zellij* patterns. Yet another beautifully proportioned fountain is found in a sunken basin at the intersection of the garden walkways. While the open paved areas are dominated by their fountains and pools, the fountain in the garden is almost hidden. Only the sound of the trickling water reveals its location, and even this sound can only be heard when one descends the stairs to the sunken garden. Through this traditional method of creating a hidden enticement, water is used both to soothe and to provoke exploration.

As in most such complexes, the main entrance does not lead directly from the street into the house, but passes through a side door leading to the terrace in front of the main building. This design decision suggests to the visitor that he is only invited to partake in the activities within the garden and that a special invitation is needed from the owner to enter the more private domain of the family.

Light wells illuminate a passageway.

RIGHT
*A high wall separates public life in
the city from private life in the* riyad.

The galleries, the sunken walkways, and the roof terrace all serve to extend the amount of time spent enjoyably in the garden. Every space is connected, yet one is rarely aware of how small the overall area is. This effect is achieved through changes of level and through the many different perspectives the garden offers.

The relatively new complex is very comfortably dimensioned to a human scale. Its design holds no significant meaning, either iconological or morphological, and it thus creates a sense of leisure rather than stimulation. Even so, Dar Batha can provide many lessons for design and for the conservation of the traditional crafts used in garden design. The buildings in this complex are conceived as pavilions in the garden, not as enclosing structures. Thus the garden and the buildings create a unified whole, allowing for great ease of use and transition between interior and exterior spaces.

The palace's high side walls and the placement of the structures to form the end walls are very effective in creating an inward-looking ambience on a relatively small site. The roof terrace for both observing the city outside and the garden inside offers an alternative understanding of the space and its relation to the city. It also provides a separate outdoor space for the women of the house when the garden is occupied by male visitors. When the cool breezes arrive in the evenings, the roof terrace becomes a very desirable space for all the palace's residents.

The use of trees that are large in scale both vertically and horizontally in such a confined area is a very effective way to announce the existence of a garden to people outside the walls of the complex. At the same time, it also creates a boundary for the roof garden as well as a roof canopy for outdoor gatherings on the terraces. Each of these design elements and solutions follows the traditions of Moroccan garden design. Because of its extremely effective use of these traditional elements, the Dar Batha complex has served as the blueprint for numerous dwellings at various scales all over the country.

Today public performances are held in the open space, which then serves as a stage. The Festival of Sacred Music is frequently held here, as are dance performances, political meetings, and academic conferences, many of which are staged underneath the large oak. Functions intended by the sultan when the garden was originally designed are now enjoyed by the modern residents of Fez.

The hope that a garden will grow with time and change to fit evolving needs of its users without resorting to a reshaping of the land or removal of the surviving trees is the ambition of every designer. With the shift from the original single use by a powerful monarch to the multiple uses required by a more open and popular democracy, Dar Batha is truly a remarkable example of re-creating the past and linking it to the future.

LEFT
Brightly painted decorations on the arcade ceiling mirror colors found in the garden.

FACING PAGE
A narrow, decorated gallery surrounds the riyad.

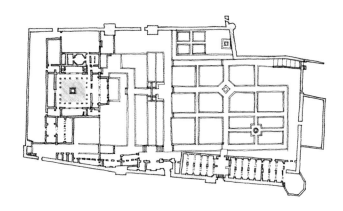

KASBAH
OF THE OUDAYAS

RABAT

The Kasbah of the Oudayas stands on the south bank of the Bou Regreg on a bluff overlooking the river estuary and the Atlantic Ocean. The *kasbah* was named after a unit from the Oudaya tribe, mercenaries sent by Moulay Ismail to defend the city and his Rabat palace following a number of violent incidents in the surrounding countryside. The wall of the stone fortification measures 2.5 meters wide and 8 to 10 meters high and encompasses the entire *kasbah*. Both the ancient wall and the old mosque in the *kasbah* were constructed by Abd el Moumen around the year 1150. In the seventeenth century, the Alawite ruler Moulay Ismail built his fortified palace on the remnants of the old wall.

The main entry point to the *kasbah* is the enormous Oudaya Gate, erected in 1195. This monumental ochre archway boasts two tall wooden doors flanked by two towers. Most of the houses along the main route to the gate were constructed by Andalusian refugees who were trying to reestablish a foothold in Rabat after they were expelled from Spain. Within the fortress are found the Jamaa el Atiq Mosque and the walled complex of the Museum of Moroccan Arts, which includes the palace, an exhibit hall, a library, shops, and an interior garden.

The main courtyard of the palace is approximately 10 meters square and is surrounded by twenty-four narrow terracotta-colored stone columns. These columns support white plaster arches, which in turn carry the heavy wooden beams that support the tiled roof. The slightly elevated colonnaded walkway and the courtyard itself are paved with square terracotta-colored *zellij*, with blue-green tiles marking the four corners of the joints and the edge of the walkway encircling the courtyard. A circular marble fountain set on a pedestal is located in the middle of the courtyard. The location of the fountain is marked by a slightly sunken

circular basin that in turn is enclosed by a green-tiled rectangular platform. Two audience chambers and two loggias face each other and open onto the courtyard, along with other rooms that previously housed the various member of the royal family.

The present garden outside the palace is sometimes referred to as the Andalusian Gardens. It was designed and constructed between 1915 and 1918 by the French colonial administration in the spirit of the original garden and was restored in 1960 by the Moroccan architect Ahmed Sefrioui. The main entrance to the building is reached by a small bridge over a moat where an old waterwheel is located, a reminder of its prior role in bringing water to the flowerbeds in the *riyad*. The garden is used today as the kasbah's public open space. The design is composed of walkways and progressively lower terraced flowerbeds, sectioned into squares. The one major allée leads from the main entrance of the palace to the secondary entrance. Another axial walkway leads to the library entrance. Fountains are located in the intersections of the walkways. Along the side of the wall facing the ocean and the cliff on which the kasbah stands, a trellis covered with grapevines leads the visitor to a more secluded area adorned with four small parterres and a pavilion located over a well. Plants in the garden function primarily to provide touches of brilliant color. Hibiscus, poinsettia, agapanthus, morning glories, marguerites, angel trumpets, large oleanders, citrus trees, palms, and few Italian cypress mix together to create a dazzling array of colors.

Even though the garden is pleasant space (much needed in the close quarters of the *kasbah*, especially today when modern living allows women to leave the sanctity of the enclosed home), this garden is missing important elements so unique to traditional Moroccan design. The simplicity of design statement, combination

*Fountains are traditionally
placed at the intersection
of two garden pathways.*

RIGHT
*A wide variety of plants add
color and texture to the garden.*

PRECEDING PAGES
View of the garden from the roof.

of function and design elements, such as the use of fruit trees as ornament or the use of water storage reservoirs to modulate the climate and water the plants and at the same time serve as the focal point of the space, cannot be found here. The intensity normally provided by the bright tiled pavement and the calming effect of the voids, the contrast between sunny, stark open space and the dark-shaded green planted areas are not compensated for by the gardens' beds and the exuberant color of the imported plants. Thus the contemplative nature of the garden, the refuge one seeks from the city, is achieved today only indoors, in the courtyards inside the museum.

While the interior courtyard of the palace shows a way to rebuild and restore open spaces in the spirit of an older culture, the garden is simply an example of the search for decorated relaxation space for today's urban dwellers. The places of the past, where spare and tightly used space provided much-needed refuge to contemplate and to center one's thoughts, do not seem to be in much demand today. The modern residents of the city are instead looking for places to congregate and for an image to replace the disappearing countryside. The garden of their desire is no longer a secluded retreat but now an outdoor meeting room where all are welcome.

RIGHT
Intricate archways frame views from a covered path into the garden.

FACING PAGE
Embellished fountain near the kasbah *perimeter wall.*

Pergola.

RIGHT
*View into the garden with the city
of Rabat in the distance.*

FOLLOWING PAGES
The necropolis of Chellah, Rabat.

Tapestry of palm plantations
and production plots bounded
by irregular paths.

AGDAL AND ARSAT

The word *agdal* is derived from a Berber word that denotes an enclosed space. In southern part of Morocco where the Berber tradition is strong, *agdal* described a site own communally and devoted to grazing. During the Middle Ages, the word came to refer to a productive estate, generally belonging to a wealthy landowner. Because irrigated land is precious, the *agdal* played a dual role as both a working farm and a pleasure garden. The *agdal* of Marrakech is the country's largest, covering more than 1,400 acres, but most *agdals* are only a few hundred acres.

By the eighteenth century, the word *agdal* came into regular use, replacing the word *buhayra* to describe the productive gardens of the sultan, as distinct from the *arsats*, which were the productive gardens within the city walls. At the time of the Almohad dynasty, there were approximately eighty gardens within the wall of the Marrakech, producing enough food to feed the citizens in case of an enemy siege. Over the centuries, with political turmoil and the changing fortunes of the city, these productive gardens fell into disrepair.

The creation of large royal and noble gardens symbolized a promise to the Arab peoples who followed the conquerors to Morocco that they would stay, and that their new cities, many of which were founded in sites not previously known for urban habitation, were intended to be permanent. Many of the gardens were begun early, right after the conquest. The first Arab kings, Idriss I and his son, Idriss II, began the tradition in Fez in the late eighth century, following the creation of the independent kingdom that had broken away from the control of the Damascus caliphate.

Establishing settled life in the desert required securing a reliable source of water, and among the most impressive works of the early rulers were the massive hydrological projects they undertook. The limited rainfall, which true to the Mediterranean climate mostly falls in winter, meant that both storage and transport of water were critical to maintaining settled life, both for agriculture and for large-scale urban settlement. Although many of the cities were located along rivers, the river flow was erratic, especially in the summer. Accordingly, great reservoirs were created to store the surplus during the rainy months for use during the more than eight months when no rain falls. These reservoirs were typically rectangular basins covering several acres, and they were surrounded by pleasure pavilions, palaces, and extensive gardens, containing mostly fruit-bearing trees that generated considerable income for the owner.

The *agdals* created landmarks along the trade routes and provided great economic incentives to invest in other projects, including the caravansaries (inns with stables), waterworks, and other, lesser gardens. With the success of these projects, residents were attracted to the cities, which began to compete for preeminence in the arts, commerce, education, and religion. The huge fixed investment provided a shared bond in the enterprise of the city, which in turn attracted further investments in houses and businesses, as well as the infrastructure to support them.

It should be noted that royal and noble *agdal* gardens were expensive enterprises to operate. Although well-maintained plantations of this sort yielded substantial incomes, they also required sizeable capital to run, especially to manage the great groves of fruit trees and the water-delivery systems that supported them. With the decline of the fortunes of particular dynasties, these gardens would often sink into a state of disrepair, forced to await the accession of a more vigorous ruler from a new dynasty who

would allow the gardens to flourish again. If, as often happened, the rulers chose a new city as their capital, the great royal gardens of the old capital would be allowed to languish, as would the gardens of the lesser nobles who would be forced to follow the court to its new home.

This phenomenon is described by Mohammed El Faïz, a civil servant who has made a career out of pressing for the restoration and preservation of the great Moroccan gardens. In his 1996 study of the gardens of Marrakech, he notes that prior to the French conquest, most of the gardens there had fallen into disrepair, and it was only relatively late in the period of French control that funds and personnel were assigned to restore them. He carefully documents the decline of the great orchards; for instance, between 1916 and 1940, as many as 30 percent of the citrus trees had died in the *agdal* of Marrakech. The decline was further exacerbated by policies that sought to promote the preservation of architecture but neglected to provide for gardens and by the diversion of water to the growing urban populations. Only after more systematic and modern methods of collecting and transporting water (deeper wells, pipelines, etc.) had begun to be installed were efforts made to restore the gardens to something of their former glory. But they remain only precariously maintained, and as El Faïz points out, without the efforts of organizations such as UNESCO, with its World Heritage Program, they may not survive the crush of growing populations and shifting political and economic realities.

There were a number of prime considerations in laying out an *agdal* garden. First, the garden should provide a strong contrast to the barren and desolate character of the countryside: it should be a place of refuge—cool, scented, and refreshing—and provide a colorful foil to the monochromatic desert. In addition to being a productive farm, the *agdal* was intended as a place to delight the senses, and all the senses were considered. One of the many terms for garden in Arabic is *bustan*, literally a place of smells or fragrance, and plants were frequently selected and bred for their aroma, especially the greatly prized roses. The colors, shapes, and varieties of plants were chosen with care, and a great deal of effort was put into the physical layout to create vistas, landmarks, and interesting patterns. Gardens were expected to attract songbirds, and the sighing of the wind provided a natural accompaniment to conversation. Tactile experience was important, as was

the quality of the fruits and vegetables that provided the tastes sought by owners whose sophistication in culinary matters marked them as refined and civilized.

Gardens were also designed as places for contemplation. Poetry is a valued and respected art in Arabic culture, and much poetry is devoted to the description of the pleasures of visiting gardens. The garden is the return to legendary Eden, to paradise within a hot and hostile environment. It is a place to observe nature and life in all their variety, from early in the morning to late at night, through the seasons and over the years as plants grow, mature, age, and finally die, only to be replaced by new ones, often generations later.

The *agdals* were also places to satisfy scientific curiosity. The rulers of Morocco made great efforts to bring new trees, shrubs, and edible plants from other regions, particularly Spain and Portugal. Gardeners and nobles alike took great pains to transplant and breed new varieties into Morocco—much as, centuries later, British colonialists did throughout their empire. Many of Morocco's most familiar plants owe their presence in areas far removed from their native habitat to these gardens and the traditions that went with them.

Finally, the gardens were places to show both the grandeur and the generosity of Morocco's rulers. Generosity has a very high place among the virtues of the desert culture from which the Arab conquerors came. To be able to share wealth was a mark of greatness. Many of these noble families would regularly open their gardens to the public; the display was intended both to impress with its wealth and to earn the praise of the masses that the owner was prepared to share his possessions with lesser beings.

Because the *agdals* are primarily working gardens, their design had first to consider functionality and the mechanics of irrigation; aesthetics are considered once the function and productivity of the garden are assured.

Walls enclose most *agdal* gardens, while others are surrounded by rows of trees. In either case, the enclosure serves to create a protected microclimate for the garden, shielding it from the harsh, dry winds of the desert. In the midst of the green open space, pavilions and kiosks are placed as spots of rest and leisure, permitting the user to experience a sensual taste of heaven.

The design of the *agdal* garden is formal, but it responds more to the site than the highly manipulated urban courtyard. In hilly or mountainous areas, *agdals* are sited on sloped terrain. Early builders responded to the site by terracing their gardens; over

time, the different elevations came to be associated with different users and uses. In times past, the lowest terrace would serve as a site for public receptions. The middle ground was the domain of the men, while the upper terrace was most private, reserved for the owner's family and the women of his household.

Most *agdals* follow an orthogonal geometry with the traditional division into four parts or multiples of four, depending on the size of the *agdal*. Long axial paths, often lined with tall evergreen trees, draw the eye into the distance, while green blocks of vegetation make a dark corridor to entice the visitor. Glimpses of kiosks, pavilions, and other structures at the ends of the paths also pull the visitor into the garden. In the planted areas, tall shade trees provide shelter for the orderly lines of fruit trees growing beneath them, which are left unprimed to shade the smaller plants below. The planted flower and vegetable plots are often sunken beneath the level of the paths, providing shade for the plant roots and allowing for flood irrigation. The smaller vegetables and flowers are often planted casually, with stems overhanging the adjacent paths, inviting the touch of visitors as they pass. Because the flowers and foliage are at the level of the raised paths, the effect is of walking on a colorful, fragrant Persian carpet.

The *agdal* gardens are planted in a wide variety of productive species. Olive, laurel, lemon, orange, almond, apricot, plum, pomegranate, jojoba, and fig orchards are found in most areas. On hillside locations where conditions permit, cooler-climate fruit trees such as quince, apples, pears, cherries, and hazelnuts are cultivated. Common vegetables include peppers, potatoes, cabbages, eggplant, and pimentos; seasonings and spices, such as mint, sage, and sweet marjoram, are also part of the garden plantings.

It is important to note that in the eastern High Atlas and the Sahara lowlands, the word *agdal* still retains its earlier meaning as a system of land management for pasturage used and owned collectively. Each village has its *agdal*, and access is restricted to the residents. Each *agdal* has it own guard, the *amghar n'ugdal or n'tuga* (the "grass guard"), to supervise the opening and closing of the pasture site and enforce the rules for the use of the land. By limiting use of the *agdal* to certain times of the year, this system prevents overgrazing and allows fallow periods for the native vegetation to regenerate, which in turn maintains vegetative cover and thus minimizes land erosion and loss of soil fertility, problems endemic to unmanaged land in the region. In the rural areas these lush *agdals* stand out as sanctuaries, living green islands in the vast arid landscape.

HOTEL MAMOUNIA

MARRAKECH

The fifteen-acre *arsat* garden of the modern Hotel Mamounia is located immediately adjacent to the west-facing wall surrounding the old city of Marrakech. Today's garden is the remnant of the thirty-two-acre estate given to Moulay Mamoun by his father, the Saadian sultan Sidi Mohammed, in the seventeenth century. The site was eventually developed into an orchard garden that became known as the Arsat El Mamoun.

The current hotel was designed by the architects Prost and Marchisio in 1922 and was built in 1923 on a portion of the site with the intention of attracting foreign dignitaries and tapping into the growing tourism industry. It quickly became the preferred place to stay for visiting celebrities and an exotic location for filmmakers from Europe and the United States. Winston Churchill, Charles de Gaulle, Charlie Chaplin, Theodore Roosevelt, Ronald and Nancy Reagan, Nelson Mandela, and numerous musicians and artists have been among the notable visitors who have contributed to the hotel's cosmopolitan reputation. Churchill's paintings of scenes from his window and the description of his impressions of the surrounding views attest to the charm of the place.

The interior of the hotel is designed in the art deco tradition, with very fine examples of this style seen in the lighting fixtures, furniture, and wall decorations. The open spaces such as the main courtyard and the garden pavilion contain excellent specimens of Moroccan craft in painted wood, metal, *zellij*, and marble created by contemporary craftsmen following traditional methods.

The hotel garden is surrounded by high walls that shield it from the city and help perpetuate the atmosphere of the paradise garden created by its original designers. Visitors reach the garden by meandering through the hotel lobby to the back of the build-

ing, catching glimpses of the exquisite green marble interior courtyard along the way. A circular fountain near the rear entrance of the hotel welcomes guests to the grounds; to the northeast of the fountain is a small formal garden, separated from the upper walkway by planting beds and a water channel. This intimate garden contains an elongated sunken pool and a central planted area fragrant with the scent of petunias, snapdragons, roses, lantana, nicotiana, and jasmine. The surrounding pathway crosses over itself, creating a figure eight that extends the opportunity for leisurely wandering in this small space. The view from the entrance of this semipublic garden terminates in a more secluded planted space around a raised fountain placed in a shallow pool paved with green and white *zellij* in a rippling herringbone pattern. The splashing jet of water falling into the shallow pool below captures the rays of the afternoon sun, illuminating this spot and drawing individuals who seek quiet solitude.

The main garden consists of a central axial walkway that begins at the hotel's rear exit and culminates at the garden pavilion set at the intersection of the secondary walkway in the middle of the garden. This position allows visitors to view the structure from all directions and creates a more private hidden space behind the structure. The burial site of an important saint, the pavilion is no longer open to visitors. Instead, three small villas were built in the garden to accommodate hotel guests' needs for private spaces for entertaining.

The visitor's view is directed from the hotel toward the pavilion by the rows of olive trees and the benches that line the crushed-stone walkway. From here one can glimpse the high walls that surround the site, towering over the pavilion and olive trees. Smaller walkways surround the entire garden, sectioning

Green tiles of various sizes and shapes form a dazzling carpet in the courtyard.

RIGHT
View through the citrus grove toward bougainvillea-covered walls.

the space into six rectilinear planted areas bordered by olive trees. Benches are located along the main walkway where strollers can sit and meditate or look at other visitors. The square plots are planted with citrus trees spaced far enough apart to allow the production and picking of fruits. Palm trees were once planted as the upper canopy, shading the orchards and protecting the more delicate plants from the scorching sun. Today most of the palm trees are gone; only two survivors remain on the horizon. A few small water channels along the walkways are planted with water-loving plants, including papyrus and water lilies. These channels are located strategically to create places to linger and dip one's hands in the cool, flowing water.

This iron gate is worked into relatively simple curves and arabesques, in contrast to the more intricate designs found in plaster, tile, wood, and brass.

FACING PAGE
Zellij with an Indian motif.

The walkways are paved with tan-colored crushed stone. The gray green of the olive trees is accentuated in the late afternoon when the wind rustles the leaves and exposes their silvery undersides. Through this grayed screen one gets glimpses of the dark green citrus trees beyond. The lighter green lawn becomes the canvas for the shifting shadows of the trees during the day. While the gardeners constantly change the flowering plants that border the walkways, the flowers are small and insignificant and do not detract from the overall lush green color scheme. Within the garden, man-made elements are rendered in tans and rosy earth colors; natural objects are predominately green in various shades. This scheme is the inverse of the color of the desert land outside the walls, where earth tones are the natural elements and the green trees are the cultivated objects in the landscape.

Thanks to the benign climate, the bougainvillea vine, a nonnative plant, has acclimatized itself to Morocco. The plant covers one entire wall with flowers the entire year round, dazzling the visitor with its blazing magenta flowers and providing the garden's strongest color accent. In March and April, the fragrance of citrus blossoms fills the air with wonderful, almost intoxicating fragrance. The clean scent draws guests out of doors during the warm days and cool nights.

Although the hotel's designers preserved much of the integrity of the original garden, they made a concession to modernity by incorporating a swimming pool, a cabana to serve as a changing room, and passive recreational space for the use of the hotel visitors. While the renovation spoiled the garden's symmetry, one can still imagine the grand simplicity of the original design.

The garden's sense of utter peace and tranquility envelops the visitor despite the fact that the hotel is overflowing with guests. The simplicity of the design, the use of limited plant materials, the muted sounds—the occasional footsteps on crushed gravel, water falling gently into a basin—keep others from breaking this feeling of repose, projecting a message to the gregarious to stay indoors or remain secluded behind the dense shrubbery and trees surrounding the hotel's play areas.

More than any other garden in Morocco, the garden at the Hotel Mamounia can serve as a prototype for an almost universal urban garden. The simple geometry, the repetition of forms, and the discrete use of plant materials allow the design to evoke an image of organized, controlled, and introverted space carved out for the benefit of those who seek refuge from the bustling social spaces in the city.

Fountains define individual areas in the garden, some secluded and others more public.

AGDAL AND MENARA GARDENS

MARRAKECH

The Almohad sultan Abd el Moumen captured Marrakech in 1147. One of his important projects was the creation and installation of the *buhayras* and *arsats* of the town, productive gardens that would feed the sultan's household and the people of the city.

In the mid-eighteenth century, Alawite sultan Mohammed III reestablished the Agdal and Menara gardens, replanting the olive groves, palm trees, and citrus plantations and restoring the dilapidated reservoirs. These monumental gardens remain in existence today, located to the south and southwest of the *medina* of Marrakech. Several other *agdals* in various stages of reconstruction exist in close proximity to these gardens on the outskirts of the town, but the Menara and Agdal have been maintained to a point where a casual visitor can appreciate the grandeur of these spaces and the power and resources that were needed to maintain such plantations.

THE MENARA

The word *menara* has several meanings, including lamp, chandelier, and minaret—all of which connote the idea of a beacon, as if a garden in the middle of the desert is a source of light, directing visitors to the place of refuge.

In 1866, Sidi Mohammed Ibn Abd Al Rahman* built a small pleasure pavilion on the eastern edge of the Menara reservoir composed of a few rooms with a two-story loggia; the retreat was surrounded by a garden of cypress, citrus trees, and flowering shrubs. The sultans and high court officials used the pavilion as a place of relaxation and entertainment.

It seems odd that the building faces west when the impressive and unique view of the Atlas Mountains and the land beyond is so strikingly displayed to the east. The explanation may lie in the attitude of the indigenous people, who for generations have grappled with the extreme and hazardous conditions imposed by local climate and topography. The shimmering water in the reservoir, the vast stretches of silver green olive trees, organized in geometrical and orderly ranks, with ribbons of channels bringing water to the plants—and thus wealth to the owner of the garden—might have provided a more valued image of strength and tranquility. Viewing the landscape that we so admire today may have been an unwelcome reminder of the treacherous desert lying just outside the boundary of this man-made refuge.

Today, the reservoir is a favorite strolling place, especially in the late afternoon when glow of the setting sun illuminates both the surface of the water and the facade of the building. Situated against the magnificent background of the Atlas Mountains, the garden and its pavilion frame a breathtaking panorama of the evening sky.

The Menara garden covers more than 250 acres and contains a water reservoir of approximately 180 by 160 meters. The three reservoirs at the Menara and the nearby Agdal garden are fed by underground systems of *khettara* and streams that are diverted toward the reservoirs. From the reservoirs the water travels through concrete and earthen channels until it reaches the planted area. The pools once served as training sites for the sultan's soldiers, who learned to swim and row boats there prior to being sent on expeditions to Spain. The sultan and his visitors also used the pools for leisurely rides in their pleasure boats. The reservoirs were stocked with large fish and small crustaceans; these creatures are still a source of delight to those who visit the garden today.

The concrete walkways surrounding the Menara's reservoir measure about 4 meters wide on the northern and southern edges

ABOVE
Entrance to the Menara pavilion garden from the agdal.

RIGHT
The immense reservoir creates a striking contrast with the surrounding arid landscape.

LEFT
*View of the reservoir, fruit trees,
and* agdal *buildings in the distance.*

FOLLOWING PAGES
*View from the Menara pavilion
across the reservoir.*

and almost 10 meters on the western side opposite the pavilion. There are several spaces that extend from the corners of this large platform that allow for more private gatherings. A series of simple stairs bring visitors up from the planted area to the corner spaces. Once paved with *zellij*, today the spaces are devoid of color. Yet this private space, elevated from the planted area but recessed from the large pool, is very inviting.

The scale of the reservoir and the elevated platform where it and the surrounded walkways are sited make the Menara a comprehensible space; as a result, it is more attractive to visitors than the much bigger and less coherent Agdal. The Menara's reservoir and pavilion constitute the center of the garden, the place where most people visit to walk and observe the landscape. The less frequented orchards and cultivated areas are used during the day for picnicking and relaxation.

THE AGDAL

Marrakech's Agdal garden is much larger than the neighboring Menara. It comprises approximately 1,400 acres, of which the two pools, each roughly the same size as the reservoir in the Menara, occupy a small part of the garden's southern portion. The smaller of the two reservoirs in the Agdal is named Sahrij al Kharsiya*, while the larger is Sahrij al Hana (Tank of Health).

Unlike the Menara, the Agdal is composed of many separate and distinct planting areas, some open to the public and others not. During the early 1940s, an inventory of the garden determined that the Agdal had more than 40,000 trees, mostly oranges and olives. Other productive trees, including plums, apricots, figs, almonds, pomegranates, and palms, were also planted in large numbers. In addition, the Agdal had more than 700 grapevines, and a certain amount of land was set aside for annual planting of vegetables, herbs such as saffron and henna, and flowers. Today the number and variety of fruit-bearing trees have been greatly reduced; nonetheless, the garden still produces a substantial harvest of crops.

At one time the Agdal was considered an extension of the Badi and Bahia palaces, the garden of the Saadian tombs, the *Makhzen*, and the Royal Palace. Other pavilions in the garden include the kiosk in the Jnan el Radwan* and the two unrestored pavilions located next to the pools. Today, the Agdal is experienced simply as a very large orchard; the relationship of the gardens to the palaces and the pavilions is only understood from above.

TOP
An individual agdal in the Drâa Valley surrounded by a rammed earth wall.

ABOVE
Agdal walkway.

RIGHT
Enclosed citrus grove in the Marrakech Agdal.

212

THE AGDAL

MEKNÈS

The building of *agdals* was not confined to the Marrakech area. During the Almohad dynasty *agdals* grew larger, and their use spread from Morocco to the wider Mediterranean region. In later dynasties, lack of finances meant a reduction in the size of the basins, but this did not deter every sultan building a new capital from finding a place for at least one major *agdal*.

Moulay Ismail turned Meknès into his capital, surrounding the city with ramparts and elaborated gates and installing enormous gardens and pools within the city walls. His "garden city" comprised more than 10,500 acres, 7,000 of which were open spaces and gardens. The only surviving pool is the *agdal* basin he built in 1674, located in a 250-acre garden.

The basin measures about 340 meters by 150 meters and is only about a meter and a half deep. As in Marrakech, the pool served as a training ground for the soldiers and a place for rowing small boats for the sultan's amusement. Ten *nurias* were installed to provide river water to the basin through a system of canals; the traditional name of the basin was Sahrij el Swani, the Basin of the Nurias. Today the basin is a focal point for the residents of Meknès. They stroll around the large pool, pick figs from the trees that sprout around it, or sit on the edge and gaze into the water and at the ruins of the great palaces in the background.

There are cisterns and basins in every place of habitation in Morocco, some small and some much bigger than those described here. The Sahrij al Kabir,* for example, in the vicinity of Fez, measures 200 meters square and is 3 meters deep. Such basins were the center of the activities of the garden even if they were not located in its geographical center; in fact, *Buhayra,* the original name of the Marrakech Agdal basin, means "small sea," a comment on its location at the garden's edge.

Maintaining the functions of the *agdals*—providing food and water, serving as campgrounds for the sultans' soldiers, and acting as a pleasure retreat—required immense resources. These gardens and basins were created and maintained to reinforce the power of the sultans and glorify their names. However, these places can also be seen as a reflection on the nature of the supreme power, which instilled in the rulers and the people the will and the ability to build them.

CONCLUSION

Form, wrote Ben Shahn, is the conversion of content into a material entity, rendering it accessible, giving it permanence. Both the content and form of gardens are abstractions, the essence of the milieu in which they are created and grow. In addition to their value in aesthetic terms, gardens require both energy and capital, making them a precious commodity.

The symbiotic relationship between nature and culture is more pronounced in garden design than in other forms of art. The garden is a multifaceted artifact, at once a canvas, a three-dimensional sculpture, a place of human refuge and shelter, and a place of work and production. The various functions of these human creations are transmitted to users through a unique set of signs and symbols. These may be subtly communicated in the choice of plants, the shape of the curves in the framing walls, the colors of ornamental tiles, or even the sounds produced by running water.

The traditional courtyards and gardens of Morocco stand as a unique example of this intricate relationship of form and content, natural conditions and human intentions. While the many levels of meaning encoded in the forms of Moroccan gardens could provide the subject of lifelong research, involving the study of religious aspects as they are understood today and the layers of historical meanings associated with the rituals and rules embedded in Moroccan culture, this book focuses on the natural and built environment in which these gardens were created, to survey the forms and materials with which they were made, and describe their functional, structural, and operational aspects. It also explores the nature of the spiritual experience aroused in those who visit Moroccan gardens, through observation and appreciation of these gardens' aesthetics, the incorporation of horticultural and agricultural expertise into the design, and the role they play in fulfilling the basic physical needs of those who frequent them.

The traditional courtyards and gardens of Morocco range from introverted postage-stamp sites to immense public reservoirs and oases. They dot the fabric of the cities, towns, and exurban areas, adding depth and nuance to the tapestry of settlements. Some courtyards are no more than air wells of bare earth; others are monumental spaces paved with ornate tile carpets. Some are lush green jungles of fragrant plants; others have become a source of life, embracing fountains that provide water for public and private use. Courtyards and gardens in Moroccan cities are as much a part of residential architecture as they are an integral part of public and commercial spaces. All of the existing examples that have been described were created to suit the extreme geographical and environmental conditions of Morocco's arid and semi-arid climate.

The main design concept of these open spaces in Morocco is, first and foremost, the concept of order. Next are the notion of privacy and the interrelation of simplicity and complexity. Gestures of separation and dispersion isolate those who experience the garden. They may be achieved by providing a vast amount of space or by carefully distributing rooms in limited space; in either case, scale is manipulated and articulated toward a desired effect.

In Morocco, the idea that nature is entirely dominated by man and a heritage of religious belief govern every design gesture. Tiled, unplanted courtyards have been used either as the center of domestic activities or as the place for the practice of religious rites. In the case of the religious place, the space itself represents

Kasbah of the Oudayas, Rabat

an abstract spiritual notion, embracing the attributes of acceptance and patience as they are captured in spatial form. Through the deployment of symbolic shapes, the play of numbers, and the ornamental use of selected texts from the Koran and verses from poetry, the users of gardens are constantly reminded of their cultural and spiritual heritage.

The forms and designs of traditional Moroccan courtyards and gardens are derived from the fusion of a number of cultural influences introduced by successive groups of settlers, each of whom built upon what earlier groups had created. The Berbers, the Phoenicians, and the Roman conquerors brought with them new habitation patterns, agricultural practices, and plant species. In the seventh century, the followers of Islam who swept in from the Arabian Desert infused the existing traditions of courtyards and gardens with a new religious symbolism. Other influential touches were provided by the Spanish conquistadors, who took the gardens and courtyards inherited from their Moorish rulers to the New World, bringing back New World flora to the cities of the Old World.

Traditional Moroccan courtyards and gardens remind us that whether rural or urban, gardens are an integral part of our human habitation, a necessity for all rather than a luxury for the elite few. The examples we see in present-day Morocco provide an important typological archive for scholars and designers. These courtyards and gardens evolved in response to environmental and cultural constraints that in many ways mirror conditions that have come to be prevalent throughout the world today: dense patterns of human settlement, dwindling water resources, depleted soils, fewer and increasingly specialized plant materials, and shortages of labor and capital for the creation and maintenance of purely decorative spaces. Yet the long-established Moroccan solutions do not betray these constraints. The gardens and courtyards of Morocco provide the visitor with a feeling of indulgence and comfort, spacious tranquility, and managed order. The materials used, the articulation of water, and the scale of the spaces are in many cases modest, yet always extremely satisfying.

These gardens offer us the accumulated wisdom of many generations and civilizations. They can teach us to balance natural systems with the requirements of human life, inspiring present-day city dwellers to create for themselves a world in which the need for ritual and artifice does not obscure their desire for a connection to nature.

ACKNOWLEDGMENTS

This book is dedicated to my paternal grandmother, Tamar, who introduced me to the wonder of Morocco's architecture and garden design when I was six years old.

I would like to thank my husband and friend, David Stein, who was the sole reason for the initiation and conclusion of this book with his patience, encouragement, and meticulous help.

Many thanks to my editor, colleague, and friend, Amy Ryan, who sifted through the pile of words, papers and pictures to help bring this book to light. Her careful questioning and editing taught me the value of clear articulation and the need to elaborate in order to convey design concepts to the public.

Many thanks to my friend, the photographer Ram Rahman, who accompanied me on my first trip to Morocco. His photographs illustrate my ideas perfectly. His social skills together with the Moroccan fondness for, and knowledge of, Bollywood movies helped open many doors that otherwise would have been closed to me.

My thanks to my former student and photographer, Albert Alvarez, who drove safely through a desert sand storm to see the fogaras of Erfoud and who photographed parts of southern Morocco I had not visited before.

I am indebted to Marcia Bernicat, former American consul in Casablanca, who hosted Ram Rahman and me in Casablanca and directed us to several sites in Salé.

I would especially like to thank all the Moroccan officials and all the people whom we met in the cities, towns, and villages in Morocco for their warm appreciation of my work. They all gave their help without reservation, despite the fact that we had no official endorsement and they knew about my origin and my nationality. Thank you all for your humanity and your open acceptance. You showed me another face of your tradition and beliefs, one that is mostly unknown to the rest of the world today.

BIBLIOGRAPHY

Ardalan, Nader, and Laleh Bakhtiar. *The Sense of Unity: The Sufi Tradition in Persian Architecture*. Chicago: University of Chicago Press, 1973.

Arthus-Bertrand, Anne, and Yann Arthus-Bertrand. *Morocco from the Air*. New York: Vendome Press, 1994.

d'Avennes, Prisse, ed. *Arabic Art in Color*. New York: Dover Publications, 1978.

Basma, Ahmed Abou. *The Imperial Cities: Morocco's Pearls*. Rome: MP Graphic Formula, 1996.

Ben El Khadir, Mohamed and Abderrafih Lahbabi. *Architectures Regionales: Un Parcours a Travers le Nord Marocain*. Casablanca: Imprimerie Najah el Jadida, 1989.

Curtis, William J. R. "Type and Variation: Berber Collective Dwellings of the Northwestern Sahara." *Muqarnas* 1(1983): 181–209.

Dawood, N.J., trans. *The Koran*. London: Penguin Books. 1990.

El Faïz, Mohammed. *Les Jardins Historiques de Marrakech*. Florence: Edizioni Firenze, 1996.

Gallotti, Jean. *Moorish Houses and Gardens of Morocco*. New York: William Helburn, Inc., n.d.

Jereb, James F. *Arts and Crafts of Morocco*. San Francisco: Chronicle Books, 1995.

Kasba 64 Study Group. *Living on the Edge of the Sahara: A Study of Traditional Forms of Habitation and Types of Settlement in Morocco*. The Hague: Government Printing Office, 1973.

Knopf Guides. *Morocco*. New York: Alfred A. Knopf, 1994.

Lehrman, Jonas. *Earthly Paradise: Garden and Courtyard in Islam*. Berkeley: University of California Press, 1980.

Lewalle, José, and Norbert Montfort. *Fleurs Sauvages du Maroc*. Robdorf: TZ-Verl.-Ges., 1997.

Menjilli-de Corny, Irène. *Jardins du Maroc*. Paris: Le Temps Apprivoisé. 1991

Nasr, Seyyid Hossein. *Islamic Science: An Illustrated Study*. England: The World of Islam Festival Publishing Company, Ltd., 1976.

Paccard, André. *Traditional Islamic Craft in Moroccan Architecture*. Saint-Jorioz, France: Editions Atelier 74, 1980.

Parker, Richard. *A Practical Guide to Islamic Monuments in Morocco*. Charlottesville, Va.: Baraka Press, 1981.

Rabinow, Paul. *Reflections on Fieldwork in Morocco*. Berkeley, Los Angeles and London: University of California Press, 1977.

Rubel, E., and W. Ludi. *Ergebnisse der Internationalen Pflanzengeographischen Exkursion durch Marokko und Westalgerien, 1936*. Bern: Verlag Hans Huber, 1939.

Shah, Idries. *The Way of the Sufi*. London, Penguin Arkana Books, 1974, 1990.

Wharton, Edith. *In Morocco*. Hopewell, N.J.: The Ecco Press, 1996.

White, F. *The Vegetation of Africa*. Paris: UNESCO, 1983.

Ypma, Herbert. *Morocco Modern*. New York: Stewart, Tabori & Chang, 1996.

INDEX

Page numbers in *italics* refer to illustrations.

Illustration Credits